THE MASTER TRAPPER COURSE

by Ralph Scherder

First Fork Publications

Butler, Pennsylvania

THE MASTER TRAPPER COURSE

©2019 Ralph Scherder

Design and layout by Rich Faler

ISBN 978-1-7330673-0-0

First Fork Publications

First Fork Publications
226 Oakvale Blvd.
Butler, PA 16001
724-822-1012

Dedication

To my wife Natalie, of course.
And to our beautiful children,
Sophia and Jude.

"Know your passion.
Follow it.
Dream it. Live it."

~Anonymous

Trapping, especially cutting edge trapping, is a journey ....

4 • THE MASTER TRAPPER COURSE

Table of Contents

An early season mink—a nice male.

Introduction

This book goes beyond the basics of set making, although there are plenty of unique sets described here. The real value of this book, in my opinion, are the insights into animal behavior. If you're looking to make huge catches, or even just improve your skills enough to enjoy trapping even more, understanding the habits and behaviors of the species you're after is a crucial part of that development.

Each trapper in this book is an expert on the topic discussed. Of course, that doesn't mean they aren't experts on other phases of trapping, too, but I tried to narrow each one down to a specific subject. Many of the ideas and techniques discussed in this book are ones I've never read in any magazine or seen in any DVD. That's the beauty of conversation. When two trappers sit down to swap stories, and they forget they're being recorded, it's possible to get down to the nitty gritty, the seldom talked about stuff that separates the great ones from the merely good ones.

More than that, though, I believe this book is fun. I enjoyed hearing how each person became introduced to trapping and how their passion for the sport grew. Readers will learn about the trial and error and dedication it takes to become a proficient trapper. Readers will also learn that there are no hard and fast rules in trapping. In fact, one of the things that amazed me while working on this project was that I could ask two trappers the same question and get completely different answers. And yet both were correct! They'd simply developed their own system and style that has helped them be successful, and there's much to be learned from each one that can help us on our own traplines.

Each interview represents roughly an hour-long conversation, and I'm extremely thankful to everyone who so willingly gave me their time. The folks in this book have dedicated their lives to trapping and studying animal behavior, and many of them perform demos at state and national conventions as well as schools designed to recruit new trappers. I'm forever grateful for their willingness to share their knowledge and passion for trapping with anyone who picks up this book.

— Ralph Scherder

Red O'Hearn explaining a mink set. He says, "It's getting to the point where if I could just be a mink trapper I would because they're easy to carry and a pleasure to put up."

RED O'HEARN
Making A Living on the 'Line

Mike "Red" O'Hearn of Northboro, Iowa, has lived a life many have dreamed about yet very few have had the courage to pursue. O'Hearn, who turned 60 in October, has been a full-time trapper/outdoorsman since the mid-1980s.

O'Hearn rarely talks numbers, but here are a few to consider. As of 2005, when his book Coon Trapping: The Untold Story, was published, his best catch of raccoons was 1,650. During one 10-year stretch, he trapped over 10,800 'coons and 1,050 mink. Those are staggering numbers. Recently I had the opportunity to talk to O'Hearn about trapping as well as insights into what it means to make a living in the outdoors.

RS: What's the difference between trapping for a living versus trapping for a hobby?

O'Hearn: It's just a hobby gone wrong. I have an addictive personality. I'm very blessed because I married my high school sweetheart and I came from a big family, so money was never in big supply. When it came time to gear up so that I could actually pull this thing off, I bought 750 1.5 coilsprings, had them laminated, put new springs in them, and all my wife said was, "Okay, now let's see some money."

What she really dislikes is that when I have money, I spend money. I'm like a drunken sailor. I would start equating cuts of meat to catches on the trapline, and I'd think this beef roast costs two mink and a muskrat. She'd say, "I wish you'd stop that." And I'd say, "Don't worry, honey, I'll go catch more money."

All these guys say they'd like to trap full time – or pursue any dream – but they don't want to give up their cushy job with a paycheck. Cindy and I live from fur sale to fur sale, and sometimes they're not very often or very good. But you make up your mind. Do you want to have money and be miserable, or do you want to do something you love and sometimes have money? You have to believe that you'll always be taken care of, like God tells you. Although, when your electric bill is five days overdue, you're thinking, "Okay, God, something needs to happen pretty quick."

RS: What species would you consider your expertise? And how have you turned that into a living?

O'Hearn: I really like to trap beavers. That's probably my best-

"But sometimes, in order to make big catches, it goes beyond the point of being fun."

paying gig right now. I travel to Mississippi to trap them and have won over many local landowners. When you go into a community, you feel like a snake oil salesman. Other trappers have told them they'd trap the beavers, but really they were after coyotes, or they didn't do whatever they said they were going to do. It's not easy being an out-of-towner. You have to prove yourself.

I like catching 'coons, but it's getting to the point where if I could just be a mink trapper I would because they're easy to carry and a pleasure to put up. Especially compared to beaver.

Most areas of the country have one or two species that you can capitalize on and make big enough catches that you can make enough money to live on. In Iowa, we have enough raccoons, and they're desirable fur. But when the 'coon market is like it is now, you just scratch your head. This is probably when you really should go get a regular job, but do you? No. Because the market could turn around any minute. When you don't know what day of the week it is, and you don't have to be anywhere at a certain time, it's a point of pride. All you know is that you don't have to be anywhere until November.

RS: In your raccoon trapping book, *Coon Trapping: The Untold Story,* you mention that you've caught hundreds of mink over the years while also catching thousands of raccoons.

O'Hearn: Mink are always around. I grew up during the first fur boom when 'coons were abundant. There were 10 or 20 'coons for every mink, but if you're trapping for a living, you want to take them all. A set designed to catch multiple species always has drawbacks compared to sets made to target one species. With mink and 'coons, if you play your cards right, you can take both at the same time because they live in the same habitat. When I first started learning to catch them, mink were bringing $30-35. They were a very desirable item.

Before I learned how to catch mink, they seemed to possess superior knowledge, but once you learn their habits, you find out they're no smarter than a muskrat. The only thing is, they're never really thick, or what I'd call thick. If I have a spot where I catch four or five, that's really good. Most spots only produce one or two, and many times none. But

I still haven't gotten over the thrill of seeing one of those bushy tails in the water. To actually catch something in a set specifically made for that animal – even if it's a possum or a skunk – is very satisfying.

And I do trap possums and skunks. When I go into the grocery store for a gallon of milk or a loaf of bread, and the checkout person tells me I owe them five dollars, they don't ask if I got the money from catching a skunk.

I get a kick out of the guys who say they get rid of all those little 'coons because they bring their average down. It's stupid, in my opinion, because if I have a 'coon that I sell for a dollar, then I have a dollar more than I would've had when I leave the fur buyer. I let the fur buyers sort out what they want or don't want. Sure, you might get $30 for a 'coon, but that might only make up a small percentage of your catch. You make a living on that average. I don't care if I have a $30 'coon all year as long as I have an $8 or $10 average. That's more important to me.

RS: When you're scouting a new location, what do you look for?

O'Hearn: For mink, I don't look for anything. I know they're there. It's just a gut feeling you get when you look at a stream. The first thing that catches your attention is probably the first spot you should investigate or set up.

Also, once you start catching them, you start building your confidence. When you're confident, you're unstoppable.

RS: Do you think someone starting out is too indecisive about where to set?

O'Hearn: They're reluctant to try things. Like Slim Pedersen once said, "If you haven't made any mistakes, then you haven't done anything in your life." Everybody wants to do everything right the first time. I don't know if that's possible. You learn from your mistakes. I've made all of them, many of them more than once. That's just part of the learning game.

The nice thing about trapping is that you're the guy who determines if you're successful. It doesn't matter what anyone says to you or about you. You need to allow yourself to be happy. When something happens, you can look at it as a negative or a positive, and if you're always looking at things as negative, and you don't allow yourself to be happy, then you're just wasting your life.

RS: What's the secret to making big catches? And how does that translate into making a living as a trapper?

O'Hearn: First, you have to have the animals. When you're out there on the trapline and things are miserable and not going well, you have to remember – this is supposed to be fun. But sometimes, in order to make big catches, it goes beyond the point of being fun.

I took some advice from a couple people in my hometown who saw me boohooing one day because I was twenty-some years old, had a wife and kids and never went to college. I had a friend there who was learning to weld at the community college on the GI Bill and he said, "If you think that way, then you're right, you're already done."

Then there was another older guy we called Coyote Joe because he specifically targeted coyotes back when they were just coming into the area. His whole year's catch might be six coyotes, but he got arthritis in his hips and he couldn't walk anymore. He thought, like many trappers do, that he was going to wait until he retired and then trap full time for a living. Well, that sounds good, and it looks good on paper because then you'll have your pension, social security, or whatever, and you're not depending on your fur check to survive. But if you wait that long to do it, you're either physically unable to do it or lose the desire to do it. You let the bus leave without getting on it. You have to do it when you're physically able and have faith that you'll be all right.

I always tell my wife that no matter what happens, or no matter how poorly things are going, that it will all work out. All of a sudden it's like a reality check and she says, "I know. I just wish…"

It's like the farmer who won a million dollars in the lottery. People asked him what he'd do now that he was rich and he said, "I'll probably just keep farming until it's all gone."

RS: What are some differences between trapping now and back when you learned to trap?

O'Hearn: We live an age of information overload. Every time you turn around, someone's giving you advice. "So-and-so says this…" Or "So-and-so says that." Pretty soon you're kneeling at your set wondering where in the heck to put your trap because you're so afraid of making a mistake.

I trapped with a guy named Terry in Oklahoma and the first day we went out to set coyote traps. He wore leather gloves and never took them off all day. He made sets, handled fur, smoked cigarettes, and kept the gloves on the whole time. At the first stop he stepped out of the truck and lit up a Winston and said, "Here's what we're going to do." And he took a cow bone and threw it onto the shoulder of the road, took another drag on his cigarette, chopped out a bed for the trap, finished his cigarette, lured the set, used his gloves to smooth the dirt over the trap, and two days later he had a coyote.

Where does that put everyone else? Who should we listen to? I've seen guys trap barehanded and catch coyotes. It all goes back to how we learned to do it. Sometimes we're afraid to try something new because that's not how we grew up doing it.

RS: What would you tell someone starting out trapping today?

O'Hearn: Join trapping associations, go to conventions, mingle with people, and don't be afraid to ask questions. If you don't understand something, ask someone to show you. With all the information available today, the learning curve has been shortened by decades. You can buy 20 years' worth of knowledge before you set a single trap and catch a lot of fur your first year.

Buy good equipment. Don't cheap out on equipment. Poor equipment will lose you money. Good equipment will make you money.

Keep track of what you're doing when first starting out. Take notes on everything so you can figure out what's working and what's not.

RS: What's your favorite thing to do in the outdoors?

O'Hearn: I had a friend who had years more experience than me, and he'd done way more, and I was standing nearby when someone asked him that question. He said, "When it's time to hunt mushrooms, my favorite thing is hunting mushrooms. When the flatheads start to spawn, my favorite thing is catching flatheads. When the ginseng starts to turn gold, my favorite thing is digging ginseng."

It changes with the season. I trap fur, dig ginseng, trap turtles, keep bees, whatever the season happens to be. My wife has always been a stay at home mom and stores and cans the food, and everything works together. You can have many favorite things, and if you want to make a living in the outdoors, you have to be multi-faceted and know that you're in charge of your own destiny.

Red O'Hearn has trapped thousands of raccoon—literally. That's a claim not many can make.

Coyotes don't work sets because they're hungry. They work them out of curiosity and competition.

JOE FENNELL

A Lure Maker's Guide to Using Lure and Bait

A common question among trappers is this: how much lure and bait do I use at a set? Another question might be: how do I know if the lure I'm using is working? Truth is, you can make the perfect dirthole or flat set, and you can make it in the perfect location, but you can diminish your chances of success by using too much lure, or by using the wrong lure in the wrong situation.

Most of us have those trappers in our lives who've served as our mentors at one time or another. Joe Fennell, founder and owner of Fur Taker Lures, has always been one of those trappers for me. Any time I've had questions over the years about how to fix a problem on my trapline, Joe has always provided sound advice, and my catch has always benefitted from it. Hopefully your trapline will benefit from some of his knowledge, too, as he sheds some light, from a lure maker's point of view, on how to use lure and bait more effectively.

RS: What is the role of lure?

Fennell: Obviously to attract the targeted animal. Sometimes a general predator-type lure will attract a variety of species. Used as an attraction most of the time at sites such as dirtholes and flat sets, lures

Joe Fennell with an eastern coyote.

A good lure is worth its weight in gold and can put a lot of fur on the stretchers.

help you seal the deal.

RS: Talk about the relationship between lures and baits.

Fennell: Lures work well in conjunction with bait, but a good bait should also be able to stand alone. Bait should be placed down in the hole, and some baits have limited calling range, which is why lures can work well with them. They can be used together or separate.

No matter what, from day one of trapping season, every dirthole I make has bait in it. It doesn't matter if it's early season or late season. I never used to do that until Charlie Dobbins told me his philosophy that bait keeps animals there longer and gives them something they want. But it's got to be the right bait. Stronger, cold weather bait that's compounded for late season can cause problems early on when the weather is still warm. Coyotes won't want to just eat it, they'll want to wear it.

In the early season, there are so many young-of-the-year coyotes that have never lived through a trapping season. They're used to having those so-called "toys" around their dens, such as bones, feathers, and scraps of hide that their mother dragged home for them to fight over and play with. If you use a bait that's too overpowering, they'll want to roll all over your set. A good, fresh preserved bait is good, though. A good lure will call the coyote to the set and the bait will keep it there longer and increase the chances of it getting caught.

RS: How much lure should you use?

Fennell: Follow the lure maker's recommendation. Most everybody will be in that lima bean-sized or thumbnail-sized amount, but you have to vary it. If it's a stronger call lure that's got some skunk in it, you might consider cutting down the amount in warmer weather or climates, or just save it for colder weather. Just use your head. If you think it's too strong, put it down in the hole and throw some dirt over top of it. Coyotes will know it's there and they'll find it.

RS: As a lure maker how do you determine the most effective amount to use?

Fennell: It comes down to the ingredients. Working so much with the ingredients, you get to know what they're capable of doing and how they interact with the fixatives. There are dozens and dozens of fixatives out there, and you just keep experimenting until you find something that provides the results you're looking for in your test holes. I've thrown out stuff that turned out to not be what I wanted it to be, but what can you do with it if you've already mixed it with something else? Sometimes you have to dump out a lot of money.

RS: Are there any lure and bait combinations you should avoid?

Fennell: Nothing really comes to mind that would be a nail in the coffin. There are four types of lures. Food, curiosity, gland, and call lures. Most baits are food-based. I like to place the bait in the bottom of the hole, throw some sheep's wool over top of it, and then put the lure on the wool. It doesn't matter if it's a gland lure or food lure or even a curiosity lure on that wool.

I'm a big believer that, for coyotes, I want multiple odors at the set. Read Major Boddicker's books and articles about lure testing. That guy knows his stuff. His studies found that it takes three or more odors at a set to really turn on a coyote. I've definitely seen

Making quality lures takes time. These ingredients have been aging for several years.

that in my own trapping experiences, too. I don't think it matters what combination you use.

I don't always put them all in one hole. Maybe make three little holes, one with each scent, or perhaps a walk-through type set where I can apply lures on both sides.

Trappers have to understand that the eastern coyote is almost never hungry. Now, I'm not talking about western coyotes because I don't know enough about them, although I'd bet it would be similar. But the eastern coyote, no matter what time of year, isn't working your dirthole because he's hungry. Ninety-five percent of the time, there's plenty of food out there and they're efficient enough hunters who have no problems filling their bellies any time they feel like it. They work sets because they're curious, or they're competitive and want to steal it before something else comes along.

RS: Is there ever a situation where the location dictates how you lure a set?

Fennell: Yes, territorial boundaries where coyote populations overlap, such as huge powerlines or where other terrain features come together. These are great areas to use gland lure or, even better, gland lure with a dropping or two. Later in the season I get away from the dirtholes and make more above-ground sets and flat sets, and a dropping with just a squirt of urine on it in a travelway is killer on coyotes.

To give credit where it's due, I first learned about the dropping set in Craig O'Gorman's book, Hoofbeats of a Wolfer, which is a classic. That set is deadly on wary coyotes because it's hard for them to be educated or become shy of a dropping or urine because they're so natural. That's how they communicate with each other. Year round I have a pint container in the truck, and if I find any droppings on my travels, I stop and pick them up. Even if you're not in a boundary area, it's good as a secondary set, especially later in the season.

RS: What kind of drawing power does a lure have? How on location do you have to be for it to be effective?

Fennell: It depends on wind direction and strength. It depends on the weather and humidity. It also depends on the make-up of the lure itself. There are so many variables that can affect the way an odor disperses throughout an area that it's impossible to give a cut and dry answer. The odor comes out of the set as a plume. Maybe it's not so much the distance that particular odor travels, but how the wind and weather cause it to spread throughout the area. Some lures will just work better under certain conditions. Look at how campfire smoke dissipates throughout an area. That's how lures travel, too.

The biggest thing you can do to make lures more effective is to make your sets with prevailing wind direction in mind. Even if you're off a little bit with your set, eye appeal could call them in, but I don't want to depend exclusively on eye appeal. Rather, I want the lure to work the way I paid for it to work. They're an asset, but they don't perform miracles, and a trapper still has to know its limitations. Make your sets so that you can take advantage of prevailing wind to spread that odor out over as great of a distance as possible.

RS: When do you start using call lure?

Fennell: Here's the thing about call lure. A lot of guys are under the impression that call lure is loud, but that's not always the case. The majority of the lures I make could be considered call lures, but they're milder. It doesn't have to be a nose-burning lure. Let the weather dictate when to use loud smelling lures. Use it in small amounts in warm weather, especially if it has skunk in it. Stick with something mild until the weather gets cold.

RS: How often should you re-lure?

Fennell: A good lure should stand up to a fair amount of rain, but if you have a real gully washer, then re-lure right away. If using just urine, which has a naturally mild odor, definitely reapply after a hard rain. You should reapply urine more often anyway.

I see guys do it all the time. If they're not having any action at a set for a week or so, they're first response is to dump more lure down the hole. That's probably what you don't want to do. Best is to stay away and let it dissipate or go to a new location and make a new set. If a dirthole isn't producing, try a flat set instead.

RS: Can you burn out an animal with too much lure?

Fennell: That can happen until things die down later in the season and the weather cools off. If you used too much lure and animals are ignoring it, they can become lure shy. Some can become so spooked you can only catch them with natural odors such as gland lure or urine. Any type of urine is hard for them to ignore because that's what they use for communication, so they don't ever really become educated to it.

If a coyote's ignoring your set because there's too much lure, then give it time to dissipate. Eventually it'll come back and work the set once it has weathered down.

I think a lot of it has to do with what they can see. For instance, they'll roll in a dead animal that reeks to high heaven because they can see what they're rolling in. But they can't see the bottom of your dirthole, so they don't know what's causing that odor. For all they know, it's some sort of stinking creature that's going to come up out of there and attack them. Nobody knows for sure what a coyote's thinking.

The biggest thing is to keep mixing things up and showing them something different. Use a variety of lures and baits at various types of sets. Use common sense and be patient and you'll catch coyotes.

Joe Fennell is the owner of J.M. Fennell Trapping Supplies and Animal Control. For more information about Fur Taker Lures, contact him via Facebook or call 724-445-7976.

Glands and urine are the universal way in which animals communicate.

In 2001 Ron and Pete Leggett caught 1,220 fox. Pete caught 601 and his son Ron caught 619 that year. That was during a 60-day period.

RON LEGGETT
Developing A System for Success

One of the first trapping videos I ever bought was Leggett's *Foxes by the Thousands,* produced by Pete and Ron Leggett, a father-son team based out of the prime red fox country of central Maryland. That video, for me, cast a whole new light on what it takes to catch large numbers. It's one thing to read about methods and see pictures in a book, but traveling along with the Leggetts as they seemingly pulled up to one double on reds after another made it look easy.

In truth, racking up large numbers of any furbearer is far from easy. But the Leggetts proved that when you break something down to its simplest form, which in this case meant targeting prime locations and developing a system, anything is achievable.

RS: A thousand red fox is a lot of red fox. How did it come to be that you and your dad made the goal to catch a thousand fox in a season?

Leggett: It all started when we were bet that we couldn't catch a fox. From that, Dad and I kept studying where a fox was most likely to place its paw when it worked a set, and almost simultaneously we discovered the ingredients to use in our lure that made the animals react the way we wanted them to react. It was a scent that would stay low to the ground and call for a long distance.

We also found the tapered step-down set to be most consistent. Originally, we made a deep step-down set where the animal was stepping down almost three inches before landing on the trap pan. That set worked but it was cumbersome to make and took so much time. Eventually, to catch large numbers, we needed to speed up the process and we changed the construction of the set to something simpler.

At first, trapping together, we'd set our traps 30 to 40 yards apart, but we noticed, from the first fox we ever got, that other foxes stayed right next to where we'd caught one. We started setting our traps side by side and right away started picking up doubles. We became so proficient at catching doubles that the same guy who bet us we couldn't catch a fox warned us to slow down because the population couldn't sustain that kind of harvest.

We had meetings with the Department of Natural Resources and numerous biologists and my dad asked them if it was possible to annihilate the fox population. They asked us what area we were covering and how many we were catching. He said we weren't hurting the population at all. He said that, barring disease, the numbers would stay strong, so we kept after the fox. We had a large population here for many, many years.

My dad passed away in May of 2004, but in 2001 we caught 1,220 fox. Dad caught 601 and I caught 619 that year. That was during a 60-day period. And the biologists were right. Barring disease, that number stayed consistent every season. One year, the parvovirus came through and our catch dropped down to around 387 foxes. We stayed after them, though, and kept trapping. Once the disease passed, fox numbers began to rebound and our catch went up again.

RS: How do you handle your own fur while also focusing on catching that many animals?

Leggett: Well, foxes were our second crop. We were dairy farmers first. We'd milk in the morning and then run traps until about four o'clock in the afternoon and then go back and milk again and then skin our catch that night. It was a ritual where you just kept going. We got very proficient at skinning. We'd stand side by side and averaged one fox every six minutes, and that included taking out the glands and putting the hide on the stretcher.

We had two nights of 50. The most we ever had in one night was 52, and we didn't get done skinning that night until 12:30. That was a long day.

We had so many foxes where we trapped. One day I radioed him and asked how he was doing. He said, "I'm doing pretty good. I'm headed home." I said, "Are you sick?" He said, "Oh, no, I'm done." I said, "Done? It's only 1:30." He said, "I know, but I'm done." I asked how many he got and he said, "21." I said, "21?!"

I might have ended up with 12 or 18 that day, I don't know. Our catches always ran with the weather fronts. My trapline was a little to the west of his, so I'd do better one day and then the next day he'd do better.

I'll be 74 in August (2019) and I'm doing wildlife control work right now and working 12 to 18 hours per day. God has blessed me with decent health.

RS: What types of locations do you look for? What catches your attention and makes a location a hot spot?

Leggett: The average farm around here ranges from 120 to 150 acres in size, but we knew we weren't trapping just that farm. We might have only two traps on that farm, but that farm would serve as a dispersal route that fox were running.

We looked at the distance between farms and how those farms connected. We looked at pinch rows and housing developments and figured out what forced foxes to travel in certain directions. Not all farms had dispersal routes on them, but that's what we were looking for when we set one up.

I taught at the Fur Takers College for 17 years and always tried to explain what a location looked like when you pulled into a field. On any farm, you'll find numerous locations that will produce a fox, but if you

Ron Leggett with a nice day's catch.

know what you're looking for, you can find that one crossing used by multitudes of fox. We never used aerial photos or topo maps, but now at the Fur Takers College, Robert Colona does an excellent job of using them to show why we caught so many animals back then.

Actually, my dad was much more proficient at picking locations than I. He had an eye for it. I had this farm I'd been trapping for a number of years and my friend said the foxes crossed by a telephone pole. Well, Dad and I were driving down the lane one day just to visit and I told him that I just didn't understand why Joe said that the foxes crossed by the telephone pole but all I ever caught there was two or three. I didn't know where they were going but they're not cutting up across this lane. Dad had me stop the truck and back up. He looked out across this flat field that had just a little bit of a draw running through it. He said, "See that fence post down there? See how that land comes up in a draw, and see how that small draw comes up beside it in the middle of the field at the end of that rock break? Set your traps at the end of that rock break."

I caught 21 fox in that location! He was amazing. He was an artist when it came to identifying that stuff. Very few people have that ability.

RS: How did you develop your trapline over time?

Leggett: Knocking on doors. That's the only way. Every time it rained or we had a free day, we'd drop what we were doing and go knock on doors.

RS: How big of an area were you trapping?

Leggett: Most of the fox we caught came from two counties and part of a third county. We were running about 40 farms per person. We each checked about 80 traps per day. Dad had a bigger loop that he ran and then a smaller loop he'd move into once he had the numbers down on the bigger one. I had two completely different lines. If farms weren't producing, I'd pull traps and move them to another farm farther down the line.

The foxes here now are being devastated by coyotes. We went through the last four years with a low population, partly due to disease, but mostly because of coyotes. Red fox populations now tend to be localized. They're being pushed into denser cover.

In my wildlife nuisance business, my calls for foxes in residential areas have increased by three or four times what they used to be with foxes under the porch or under the wood shed. They can't coexist with coyotes because of territorial dominance.

RS: How many miles did you typically cover in a day?

Leggett: We averaged 80 to 100 miles per day.

RS: That's not as many as I thought you were going to say.

Leggett: Well, you have to consider that we were milking cows and had a large population of fox. There are other trappers out there who have all day and can run traps for half the night. If he's willing to work hard, he can almost do on his own what Dad and I were doing combined. We did our farm work and then went to check traps.

When we went to Texas, we ran 150 miles per day trapping coyotes because we had all day to do it. We ran daylight to dark and didn't have a herd of cows that needed milked at the end of the day.

RS: In your lure business, you don't offer a huge variety of scents for predators. Rather, you have just a couple of lures designed for fox and coyotes. Some lure makers offer a long list of options.

Leggett: Think of it like a production line in a factory. You have a system that is very proficient. Whether it be lure, set construction, or location, it's a system based on proficiency. What we have is a set that is consistent, and a lure that is consistent, and if you want numbers, be consistent in using it.

When you go out there and throw 10 to 15 traps on a farm with a bunch of different lures, all you're doing is hurting yourself. You set that farm up with one location, and one specific lure, and they'll just keep coming once you get them started. They'll come from that big tree on the hill where you might've set and they'll follow the trail of the other fox to

Ron and Pete Leggett with their 2001 catch of 1,220 fox.

that one good location. It's a system that, when you've got it figured out, you have to be consistent when using it.

Now, a smart fox that's educated to a foot trap – or educated to a dirthole, I should say – will come in and dig you out. And they'll dig you out every time they come back. I usually move the trap around or use a second trap and catch him anyway.

But when you've got coyotes, at least here in the east, I diversify my lure. I'll use our lure first. And if I have a coyote problem, I'll try someone else's lure. I also have another lure I make that I don't advertise.

In Texas, all we used for coyotes was our lure. My dad won a world championship with that coyote lure. But when you have a smart animal, being able to diversify and try other products isn't a bad thing.

RS: What are your thoughts about human scent on the trapline? Does it discourage animals from working a set?

Leggett: Human scent will affect you over a two or three day period. As long as you don't go back there and reapply your human odor, the set will start to work. If the animals are there, that is. They've gotta be there to catch them.

RS: What was it like trapping with your dad?

Leggett: We both started trapping at the same time, when I was 17. I didn't teach him anything and he didn't teach me anything. We learned together. That's why I stopped by and visited his grave the other day for

Doubles? Here's a double double—a quadruple! Talk about major trapline production!

Ron's mom next to a red fox double in typical Maryland farmland.

the first time in 14 years. I haven't been there because it breaks my heart to know I've lost my best friend. He was my best friend first, and then my father.

I stayed with him, took care of him, and he died in my arms. I just loved the guy. He had the personality about him that he never smacked any of his children or hollered at them. When he spoke to you, it was, "Hey, Ronald, you don't need to be doing that." And that's all he had to say. He raised four children and he was an awesome father. Not everybody was as fortunate as we were.

My mom's still around. She's 94 now and still goes on the trapline once in a while. She used to love traveling around to the trapping conventions. My wife Betty was always right there with us, too. Our ability to run the trapline every morning was due to all the support that our wives and family gave us. Without their support, it would have never been possible to make the catches that we made. If we were trapping land or water, they never complained about Dad and me being gone all day.

For more information about the Leggett brand of lures and trapping supplies, visit www.TrapLeggetts.com.

"Mink trapping is a worthy pursuit."

DON POWELL
The Mink Professor

D on Powell, 55, is the founder and host of Minktoberfest, an annual event that could be considered a sort of "Woodstock for trappers." This weekend-long rendezvous draws trappers from around the country to his property in Punxsutawney, PA, to exchange ideas and knowledge while forging friendships in the outdoors. He has also produced a video and book about mink trapping and runs the website www.MinkTrapping.com. Powell is currently Vice President West of the Pennsylvania Trappers Association.

RS: Who introduced you to trapping?

Powell: When I was 9, we were visiting my granddad one Sunday, and for some reason he told me there was a #1 longspring, which he referred to as a "rat trap," down in the feed room of his general store. I asked if I could have it. Something had spurred my interest in it. Once I got that trap, I found out that one of my brother's friends liked to trap muskrats. He took my brother and I along with him, and I've been hooked ever since.

RS: Tell me about your first mink catch.

Powell: While muskrat trapping, I'd caught a mink accidentally in a 110 Conibear set in front of a muskrat hole. It was just neat knowing that mink were around. I'd never seen one in the wild before. A couple years later, I went to a convention in Dayton, Pennsylvania, and met Kermit Stearns. After talking to Kermit and following his advice, I started catching them on purpose, and that gave me great satisfaction.

RS: What do you like most about trapping?

Powell: I like the time of the year and getting out in the fall. I like seeing the deer and squirrels and seeing how things change from year to year with your set locations. I like to think I'm helping keep things in balance, too.

As a kid, there was nothing better than the financial rewards. I was making big money in the late-70s catching fur. But, as time wore on, it became about a lot more than making money. It's about the camaraderie, sharing stories with other people. I like all the species, not just mink. I like to see tracks and try to determine why that animal crossed a log, when it happened, and where it was going to. The mink is just such a resilient little fella that can come and go through the smallest cracks and crevices. It can take care of itself against any type of predator. Mink trapping is a worthy pursuit.

RS: How long have you worked in real estate?

Powell: I started in college and worked for a company. After a few years, I decided to start my own real estate agency. That was thirtysome years ago and it's been growing ever since.

RS: How did Minktoberfest come about?

Powell: After I started MinkTrapping.com, we started developing a little community. Everybody's welcome, and it's not about just mink anymore with guys like Russ Carman, Slim Pedersen, Mark Zagger and so many others coming from all over. It's grown into a great source of trapping knowledge.

It started when I invited four guys from the website to attend the first time. We went out and looked at streams and talked about techniques and set locations. It just grew from there. This will be our 10th year, and we have a great lineup of people coming.

Rich Faler's mink trapping book was a work that inspired me. Jim Spencer's was another good one. The quality and presentation of the content encouraged me to write one, too. As I went to more conventions and met people, and MinkTrapping.com took off, Minktoberfest grew along with it. Now we're maxed out at 120 people coming this year.

Minktoberfest is something that I couldn't do alone. My wife and my office staff do a great job of pulling it all together and making it a success.

RS: In many ways, the Minktoberfest slogan sums it up perfectly: "Digging the Well Deeper so that Others May Drink."

Powell: It's important to give back to the trapping community. So many people in the industry have been so good to me. They've helped me get to the point where I'm at. I've learned a lot about business. It taught me to talk to people, to be appreciative, to not take things for granted, be willing to say thank you, treat people with respect and develop relationships.

It also teaches you to get up every morning and not just let things go. It teaches you to adjust, try to make things a little bit better and pay attention to details. You only get out of it what you're willing to put into it. That's the biggest thing, in trapping and in life.

RS: What are some of the long-held beliefs of mink trappers that aren't necessarily true.

Powell: Well, mink don't "always" do anything. The answers to most questions about mink trapping could very well begin with "it depends." For instance, from my trail camera studies and just following tracks in the snow, I've learned that they don't always hug edges, despite what many of the method books in the past have said.

Charlie Dobbins once said that to catch most animals, start with a hole. But, for mink, I think you can start with a tunnel. Let's say you have a bridge wall that doesn't have many features or much to offer. A mink may typically run down the center or go wherever it wants to, but if you can make a quick tunnel, which is made by leaning a flat rock against a vertical edge, you can give them a destination to shoot for. As

I progressed, I started using the longer railroad plates and leaning them against the bridge wall or some other vertical edge. Sometimes I even use a stick to position the plate away from the wall and put some grass on top to give it more eye appeal. Now I've created a destination, a tunnel, that mink will want to check out.

Mink are easily distracted. If they're going through a featureless area, they're drawn to that quick tunnel. In the snow you'll see their tracks going right to it. The nice thing, too, is that when you put the trap in behind or underneath that tunnel, you can avoid catching most raccoons. 'Coons typically go around the set, so you could set a trap on the outside of the tunnel to catch them while still keeping your mink set working.

RS: Do you use bodygrips or footholds in the quick tunnels?

Powell: Usually a foothold in that set. The bodygrips, though, can be quick tunnels in and of themselves, depending on the stabilizer you use. Draping some grass around the open jaws can create a tunnel, too.

RS: What other behaviors have you noticed from observing and studying mink?

Powell: They're very good swimmers. The first time I saw a mink swimming, I noticed air bubbles in the water. That's air coming out of their fur. Shaking off allows that air to get back into the fur and gives them more control and buoyancy while swimming. They're also very

Don Powell enjoying one of the events at his Mintoberfest.

accomplished at turning over rocks, eating crayfish and tracking down minnows. They love eating snakes.

They're turned on by eyes. Their path of approach can be manipulated by the way you place a fish head at your set. If you have a fish head or a muskrat head in a box with the eyes facing the back, the mink will want to come in through the back. The mink will approach from whatever direction the eyes are facing, so in your mink boxes, it's important to have the head facing out.

Mink have short legs, which also impacts their approach. Whereas canines will step over things, such as a guide stick, mink will actually step on them. In the past, we were taught to use stepping sticks, but in my videos, the mink will often step up onto the guide stick and then over the trap. Bob Best taught me to use a V-shaped stick, such as a branch from a maple tree, if I need to use a guide. Push the stick in the ground and place the trap in front of the V. This prevents mink from stepping on the stick and forces them to pass through the V and hit the trap pan.

Those short legs make a big difference. With that low belly, they don't want to step over things. Whereas you want to have your trap pan lower when canine trapping, you actually want it higher for mink.

RS: Do you swap out the trap pans on your footholds?

Powell: Yes. I use the Barker Mink Pans and the Mike Kelly Mink Pans.

RS: What's your favorite foothold trap?

Powell: The old #2 Victor coilspring square jaws, although I do have a number of Duke 1 ½ coilsprings that I've modified, too.

RS: In your book and video, you describe a lot of different mink sets. What are your favorite ones to make?

Powell: I like culvert blind sets and pocket sets. Years when we have lots of high water and freezing occurs, it hard to keep those pocket sets working. I also like baited bottom sets, which is a bodygrip with a type of bait on the trigger. It can be any type of bottom edge set, down where the mink are swimming You can place a swim bait on the trigger of your bodygrip and make a very deadly set, but it's important that the swim bait has good eyes on it. Mink just can't resist hitting it.

My 'line is a progressive 'line. I try to get 2-4 sets out per stop on first day so that my competition sees that I'm there. As the season goes on, I add different types of sets to each location. I might set 4 blind sets at the corners of a bridge or culvert. The next day I may add a pocket set or two. Once I have my whole 'line laid out with blind sets and pocket sets, I then go back and start adding the baited bottom and bottom edge sets, mink boxes, and other sets. I'm basically building the 'line a little at a time.

RS: Do you do a lot of preseason work?

Powell: I'm big on preseason work. For me, my catch is usually a result of how much time I spend preparing for the season. I can go to the deepest round culvert where there's the perfect blind set, and I have a stabilizer platform with me that will fit that culvert perfectly because I took the time during the offseason to build what I needed.

I grew up carrying cement blocks to build up platforms for the trap to sit on, because those top-edge sets are very good. But now, I have much simpler tools. I get accused of carrying too much stuff on the trapline, but every tool serves a purpose. The tools I use most are platforms in many varieties. I have platforms that allow me to adjust my trap based on water conditions and levels, and they're all custom built prior to the season.

RS: What do you look for when building your trapline?

Powell: I primarily run an auto 'line now, so I'm looking at culverts, bridges, any trickles near the road, and ponds. I not only look at that specific location, but also try to understand where the water's coming from and where it's going. Habitat's really the key. I might be trapping a low-cut pasture that doesn't look like a good mink area, but if there's some swamp above it or a good watershed, it can still be a good location.

RS: Can you talk a little bit about how you lay out your trapline?

Powell: I usually have 6 to 8 loops I can trap, all of which begin and end at my house, and I'll run two or three of those loops at a time. Depending on my schedule, I may run two in the morning before work and then one after work.

I prefer small water over big water, but I like to find roads that parallel bigger waters so that I can catch those tributaries flowing in. I don't set a lot of locations along each waterway. Given the choice between two locations on one stream versus trapping two different watersheds and

Some of the on-location instructions at Mintoberfest.

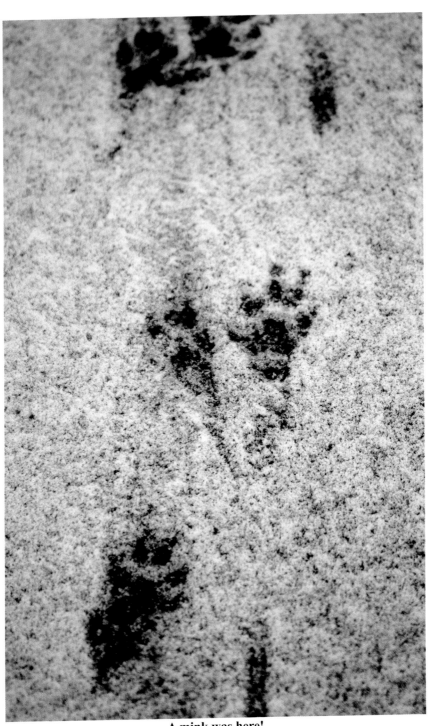

A mink was here!

having one location on each, I'd rather trap the two watersheds. That gives me access to more populations of mink.

RS: How long do you keep your traps in a location if you're not catching mink there?

Powell: I had a really minky location that was a culvert with good habitat above and below it. I found mink sign. I trapped that location for a couple of years but never did very good. Even though it looked like what I was doing should've been working, I analyzed it more and changed things around and moved my sets a little bit. The one side of the creek was a little hard to get to. The current was swifter over there and it didn't look to me like the place where mink would travel. But once I added a trap on that side of the creek, I started catching mink there.

People can give up on locations because they're not catching anything, but I think, instead of giving up, they just need to keep adjusting until they find what works.

We don't have a high-density mink population in this area of the state, which is proven by the work I've done with trail cameras. I can have trail cameras out trying to study mink all year and sometimes I'll go months in some of my better locations without even catching a glimpse of one. And then, as the season goes on, the buck mink start to travel more, so you can't give up on a location. How much they move depends on time of year, weather conditions, water levels, food sources and other factors.

The ideal weather is anything stable, whether it's freezing, warm, or whatever. But that's not what we get in Pennsylvania, so you have to be able to adjust.

RS: How do your methods change from early season to late season?

Powell: Late season, I try to have everything set up for freezing temperatures. A lot of my pockets won't be working, so I focus on dry land trails and baited boxes. I look for current where the traps won't freeze up as quickly.

Wind chill is a big thing to consider. A lot of people say bottom sets produce better when it's stormy out, but I've found they produce best when the wind chill factor is really cold. Mink get in that water, which is warmer than the outside air temperature.

RS: What advice would you give new trappers?

Powell: Just to enjoy themselves. Also, realize they're providing a service to the animals and to sportsmen by helping to control and keep populations in check. It's important to step away from the rat race of everyday life and get back to nature.

Austin Passamonte with winter weather muskrats.

Austin Passamonte
Muskrat Fever

A ustin Passamonte, 54, of Geneseo, NY, has authored numerous trapping books, all of which are excellent reads. The first animal he ever caught was a raccoon when he was only 8. Two years later, his uncle bought two brand new Conibears and showed him how to set them in the pond by his house, where they caught muskrats. Those successes fueled a lifelong passion for trapping and the outdoors.

RS: Who got you interested in trapping?

Passamonte: A couple of people. My father's older brother. Before the advent of the Conibear trap, he'd trap muskrats locally on the Genesee River with #1 Stop Loss traps. Also, my grandfather had some old, triple clutch Triumph traps in the shed that he used for marauding raccoons. Seeing those traps, and seeing those woodchucks and raccoons being caught intrigued me. And then a family friend, his name was John

Austin's favorite furbearers are muskrat and red fox. Here's a nice catch of reds.

Magel, was a major longliner here in New York and other states. Early exposure to all of those guys got me interested in trapping. After that, I was mostly self-taught. I walked countless miles just studying animal tracks.

RS: What's your favorite animal to trap?

Passamonte: I like all species, but it would be a toss-up between muskrats and red fox. Some years, in this region, muskrat populations are up and red fox are down, and vice versa. The biggest factor is the time commitment involved with each type of trapping. Land trapping in much more involved. It can take 6 days to establish a good 'line, whereas with muskrats, you can set a bunch of traps today, check and pull them tomorrow and be equally successful. That's the main reason I've been doing more muskrat trapping, because of the time convenience.

RS: For the time you spend trapping, you sure put up a pile of muskrats every year.

Passamonte: I live in an area that has a fair amount of water and a fair amount of habitat. If the water tables are right, our population is thick. If we have a summer drought and/or rough spring floods, there are very few 'rats. That's the case in most states these days. This year, we happened to have a big population, so it was fun.

RS: The nationwide trend has been that muskrat populations are declining. What are your thoughts on that?

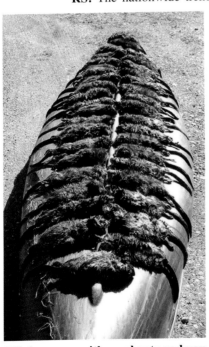

Passamonte: Our DCNR biologists did a study about a decade ago on muskrat reproduction and mortality, and for several years I was a part of that. We would sort out the females, freeze them, and turn them over to the biologists so they could do a placenta count. They also went around to various fur sales and noted the ages of the muskrats being sold, which you can tell by the stripe patterns on the hide whether it's a juvenile or adult. They compiled all these statistics and what they found was that muskrats were reproducing at equal or greater rates than they ever had. So it's not an issue of them being sterile or not being there. It's more of a survival issue. From the time they give birth until fall, those juveniles just don't survive.

I think there are a number of reasons for that and they're all

Fill the canoe with muskrats and you have to starting tacking them to the bottom!

intertwined. You can't separate one from the other. But it all starts with water. If they have a sufficient, stable water level that doesn't blow up to flood stage and then drop to drought stages, they can handle everything else. They can handle predation and pocket diseases. But if you take away the water, they can't handle anything. That's the crux of it all.

In most states, modern farming practices, clearing land, and dredging ditches are all about drainage and flood control. The habitat degradation caused by those practices is the major issue, in my opinion.

RS: How much of a factor are the expanding populations of owls, hawks, and other raptors?

Passamonte: They would be secondary factors. Take away the water and muskrats have to try to live in shallow water conditions, get up on the banks to feed more often, and now they're much easier prey.

For example, in the Finger Lakes Region, the Montezuma Wetlands Complex is 9,000 acres, and fur buyers know that some of the best muskrats come from there. It's also a bald eagle refuge and is on the migratory path of every raptor traveling back and forth from Canada. Predators hammer the heck out of the muskrats there and yet there are untold thousands of muskrats there year after year because the water levels are stable and controlled. Moral of the story, give them habitat and they can out-breed everything else. But take away the habitat and they have no chance.

RS: Speaking of drainage ditches, sometimes I see photos from your trapline and it seems like you're pulling muskrats out of thin air. The places you trap don't always look like typical muskrat habitat.

Passamonte: Well, those are places where there is stable water in the summer, and then in the fall, the road crews come around and dredge them out so that when water levels rise in the winter, ice jamming won't be a problem. Some of those ditches that look too shallow for 'rats are actually two feet deep or more early in the fall. Had I not trapped those 'rats prior to the dredging, they would have all been winter-killed. They wouldn't have survived.

RS: You're very active on social media. Do you find there's somewhat of a trapping community online?

Passamonte: Before Facebook, message boards were popular and everybody kind of congregated there. It's more scattered now. There are untold numbers of trapping groups on Facebook, and more added every month. So it's not as concentrated as it once was.

RS: How do you think trapping's image is impacted by social media?

Passamonte: In general, everybody having access to social media, having access to a camera and being able to post things that can be interpreted in a number of different ways is not good at all. News has become propaganda. In particular to the trapping industry, it can be used the same way. We communicate, learn, and interact with each other just like we're sitting around at a convention, but these things are often viewed by the public and can be misinterpreted. That's the negative side.

The positive side is that there's a large amount of good, factual information online. It's so much easier to get a proper education now. I think back to the days when I started trapping. For example, older guys who never really trapped would tell you to nail a dead chicken to a tree and set a trap under to catch a fox. Well, obviously that's a disaster waiting to happen. Nowadays, if somebody wants to learn how to trap, they go to You Tube, Facebook, do Google searches, and go to message boards and they get better, factual information by far. Everything in life is a double-edged sword.

RS: Where do you see the future of trapping?

Passamonte: It depends on two factors. The level of interest and fur prices. The motivation to hunt turkeys or deer or other species is to harvest an animal, tag it, and share the experience with your friends. Trapping is different. The reward, the measuring stick at the end of the season, is the fur check.

Also, trapping is unlike hunting and fishing in that trapping is an extended amount of work. If you want to go ice fishing, you go out today and catch whatever you catch, come home and clean it, and that's it. That was your experience. Trapping is a days or weeks or months work commitment. In life, we expect to be rewarded when we work, and the reward in trapping is the fur check. That's over-simplifying it, and I'm not trying to talk down anyone, but if the fur prices aren't there, the level of interest isn't either.

Society is changing, too. We're not an outdoors, active society. We were a lot more rural years ago and fur prices were a lot more attractive.

RS: How do you find places to trap muskrats?

Passamonte: This year, I was in creeks and ditches that I haven't looked at in 30 years. There wasn't the water that there used to be and there weren't nearly the 'rats that there used to be, but there were some. To answer your question in particular, when you look at water in muskrat season, there's going to be obvious sign. You only set on fresh sign. If you're looking at roadside ditches and you see a defined, sharp-edged channel, and maybe some fresh cuttings and den holes, then you know muskrats are there.

If you look in that ditch and the bottom is flat and silty, no defined runs or channels or cuttings, then there's nothing there. Muskrats leave a lot of sign. Many good muskrat trappers driving along can just look at a body of water, without even seeing a hut, and tell right away whether or not there will be muskrats there. It's just a matter of experience from a lifetime of looking at water that did not have muskrats.

RS: What are some of the contributing factors that you look for?

Passamonte: For example, there's a marsh or a slough that has a number of muskrat houses on it. And then you go up the road a little bit and there's an inlet or an outlet to that body of water. If it has decent habitat, such as wet, grassy areas, slow flows, blue stem grass, bulrush stands, cattails, or whatever the regional feed is, there will be muskrats in that inlet, outlet, or both.

If there's not a lot of food there, you're working with a sparse population. Depending on the terrain, it's either worth your time or it's not.

Several years ago, when fur prices were up a bit, I went out to North Dakota in the spring of 2012, before they had the historical drought. I'd drive along and see sloughs with 30, 50, 100 muskrat houses, and then I'd go to a reservoir where there were no cattails, no grass, and no habitat. You could look at the culvert and see stones with 'rat droppings, but it's not worth your time to work around that reservoir and glean a few muskrats when there are so many potholes and sloughs that are just stacked with them. But if you don't have those sloughs, and all you have are those reservoirs, then you just work with what you got.

RS: Have you ever scouted a place and then returned during the season to find the muskrats all gone?

Passamonte: Yes. It could've been from unstable water conditions, disease, other trappers, or maybe they just moved. Muskrats are a dynamic population that moves around.

RS: How much do they move and migrate?

Passamonte: When you have a big marsh that has muskrats in it one year and none the next, guys automatically think it was over-trapped and they should've left some for seed. But that's not always the case. It's those smaller sloughs, the roadside ditches, the creeks that used to flow through cropfields, the little high ground potholes that used to be in these spring flows. These smaller bodies of water that connect to the big bodies are all part of the habitat. They'll move into small bodies of water

Muskrat heaven!

in spring and summer, have their litters, and then move into the bigger, deeper flows as cold weather comes. If a pond or pocket of water loses its population, it will replenish in the spring when they shuffle. That's nature's way of filling the void.

But when you eliminate those small, connective bodies of water, those bigger ones become an island. And when they lose their population, there's nothing left to shuffle through and replenish the population. They're very dynamic. They'll live somewhere until their food or water runs out, and then they'll leave.

RS: What's your favorite way to trap muskrats?

Passamonte: In a shallow ditch where there's just one little run and I can wear my Muck boots!

When I talk to canine trappers about muskrat trapping, most of them get insulted when I say that muskrat trapping is by far the most aerobically physical. Anyone who's ever longlined for muskrats will tell you it's the most physical of all because of the constant bending and moving. Beaver trapping is exhausting while you're carrying beavers. Muskrat trapping is exhausting from 10 hours of non-stop movement and slogging through marshes while carrying loads.

In late fall through mid-winter, muskrats are oriented to swim on the bottom, which is why there are channels through marshes and ditches. That's why there are dive holes. They spend a lot of time on the bottom. That's where bodygrips shine, unless you're in a place that allows trapping at or around the huts and feed beds. Where I happen to live, it's illegal to set within 5 feet of a house. Colony traps are also illegal, but if you live in a state where you can use them, I'd drop one colony trap in a ditch instead of setting 5 or 6 bodygrip traps and move on. What I do is dictated by what I'm restricted to do.

If restrictions weren't an issue, I'd use both bodygrips and footholds and set everything. I'd set the slides on the houses, the feed beds near each hut, the big community feed beds, and I'd set the visible runs with bodygrips or colony traps. But where I live, the bodygrips in runs are the most effective. That changes a little bit in the spring time when muskrats move up from swimming on the bottom and spend more time near the surface. Now it becomes a foothold game. You're looking at locations where they crawl out, leave droppings, create scent posts and toilets.

RS: How effective are muskrat floats?

Passamonte: They're very effective for a short period of time. In our region of the state, the season is open until April 15th. Floats work best right at ice out, just as the ice is breaking up and leaving. As soon as that ice melts off, muskrats resist climbing on the floats. They just don't do it as much as they crawl onto land and create toilets.

Other places in the country, and in Canada, floats are effective for a longer period of time, and I have no idea why. I know guys in Manitoba, Canada, and all they do is set floats with 2 footholds on each one, and they'll catch hundreds of 'rats. But around here, if you set a hundred floats, you'd catch 5 or 10. Maybe.

RS: Advice for new trappers?

Passamonte: Relax and enjoy the experience, and don't expect to have success right away. We live in a world of instant gratification. Society has conditioned us that believe that, since so much information is available, once we have that information we should be able to succeed. Well, you may have the information, but you don't have the knowledge. There's a vast difference between information and knowledge – and skill, which is just knowledge applied. Of all the outdoor sports, trapping requires the most patience to master.

Just enjoy the moment. Every always preaches about the "good old days" or that things were better in the past. But it's good enough right now. Go out and enjoy what's available right now, and then do it again next season. Things change, life changes, and you never know how long you'll be able to enjoy what you are. For me, trapping is about stepping back and living in the moment, and it's about a lot more than how many I caught.

RS: You enjoy all phases of the outdoors.

Passamonte: I do. You know, it's almost blasphemous for a serious trapper to say they do anything other than trap, because trapping is all year. If we're not trapping, we're supposed to be getting ready for next trapping season, but that's not the case with me. I love deer hunting and spring turkey with a passion. If somebody told me that we could go hammer muskrats for a week or we could go to whitetail mecca and see some 150-160-inch bucks, I'd have a tough time deciding which to do. As I was an up-and-coming trapper, I was also an up-and-coming hunter and fisherman. I enjoy it all.

Give muskrats habitat and they can out-breed everything else. Take away the habitat and they have no chance.

Ed and his partner skin an average of 12 coyotes a day.

Ed Schneider
One Square Mile

E d Schneider, owner of Kansas Trapline Products, has been trapping since 1970 and making and selling his own line of lures and baits for over 30 years. Although his early years primarily focused on raccoons and muskrats, he has developed into one of the top predator trappers in the country today.

RS: What do you consider your expertise?

Schneider: As I've been trapping, going from state to state, I've learned how to get permission on property that not only has a couple coyotes on it, but will draw in more coyotes once I've harvested the first group. My book One Square Mile builds on these principals. I have a knack for finding dispersal areas. The second thing I bring to the table goes with what Craig O'Gorman writes about in Hoofbeats of a Wolfer. I took instruction from Craig and he talks about the importance of whacking the entire pack. My skill set has been developed with the intent of accomplishing that task.

We can talk all day about a saddle, or gate opening, or field corner, or crop change. But as trappers, we need to understand how this gate opening connects to the next corner of the field and to the next crop change and how they all tie together, and once we do, we're basically ambushing these coyotes over and over again. That's how I get six coyotes in a day off of one piece of ground.

Typically, I'll get six the first day, and then I'll get one or so each of the next couple of days, and then all of a sudden, around day four or five, I'll get six more. But not every property has that potential. Sometimes you have to know when the one coyote you got was all you're going to get and move on.

RS: What do you look for in a dispersal area? Are you looking for terrain features?

Schneider: In a world without fences, buildings, or human encroachment, the natural dispersal zones are wet and dry drainages. It could be a creek or river or other drainages that are part of that watershed. Animals use those drainages just like a road map, just like me driving down Interstate 70. Those are also the areas that have more habitat. Brush grows in those drainages, the scrub brush and grasses that attract prey species.

Some drainages can go on for hundreds, if not thousands, of miles. Those drainages are exactly how the mountain lions are coming out of South Dakota and infiltrating other parts of the country. That's also how the wolves will disperse into other areas.

Once we figure out the drainages, we tie in another feature, the divide that separates drainages. That divide is valuable because coyotes will run that divide as well as cross it through natural saddles. So those are the two most important features to look for no matter where you live, whether it's the Flint Hills, Rocky Mountains, or even the Appalachian Mountains. They all have very defined drainages that are easy to spot.

RS: Is elevation a factor?

Schneider: A divide can be as subtle as two feet. It may not necessarily be a big division or high elevation, but it's there. When we get into flatter terrain, we start paying more attention to landscape features. If it's flat and relatively featureless, and we have a grove of trees with some grass, that grove suddenly becomes much more important.

A good example is western Kansas where there are a lot of drainages that are very subtle. Most of the time, those drainages are pasture related. So just because an area lacks defined features doesn't mean we can't catch coyotes there. It just means we have to pay more attention to the features that are present, such as crop changes.

The thing about out west is that there's such a moisture deficiency that they don't do fall tillage on their crops, so where the wheat meets the milo would be a key spot. You need to understand, though, that crop line edge cannot support a million coyotes, but it can support a pair of coyotes. Once you catch one or two, you learn to pull the trap. In the Flint Hills, on the other hand, where there's fantastic habitat, coyote populations are much higher.

I met a guy who was a good trapper, caught around 40 coyotes a year, and after reading my book, he realized if he wanted to catch more, then he needed more coyotes. The next year he expanded his territory and caught 100 coyotes. You can't catch what's not there, and coyote trapping requires a lot of ground.

RS: I've heard you mention about learning how to get permission to trap good properties. What's your approach for asking permission to trap?

Schneider: You've got to be prepared to hear the word "No" and be just like any salesman who shrugs it off and moves on to the next property. Also, if you can't look at an area and understand where the landowner is coming from, that's a big disadvantage to you.

In trapping, we have to know the animals we pursue, their habits and behaviors. Asking for permission is similar in that you have to understand who you're talking to, what are their priorities in life, and to some degree imagine their viewpoint of the world. For instance, one of my trapping partners, Richard Johnson, is an Iowa farmer. There's no doubt in my mind that he's the right guy to talk to other Iowa farmers because they have a lot in common. I also have a farming background, which helps. You have to learn how to talk the language and know when

Sometimes you have to know when the one coyote you got was all you're going to get and move on.

not to pry too much.

If I'm trapping cattle land, then I talk to those landowners in a much different way. We talk to the cattlemen about what we can do in regards to predator control and how our services can save him money. I had a farmer in western Kansas who lost $10,000 worth of calves last year to coyotes.

We approach the grain farmer a little differently. We tell him we can trap the beaver that have dammed up the stream that's flooding his fields, or that we'll trap the raccoons that are eating his corn. And then you have to follow through, of course, and do what you tell them you're going to do, but this can also open up a lot of land for coyote trapping. We try to look at it from their viewpoint and what we can bring to the table that makes them money in the long run. We're offering them a service and we both win in this scenario.

I'll finally add that maturity goes a long way. Show up as a business man, not as a hick, and remember that you're making a business transaction. I know that doesn't fit the bill with everybody, but it sure doesn't hurt. Present yourself as a professional. If you do get permission, and you're doing a good job, there's a good chance that landowner will get you more land to trap.

RS: Once you're on a property, what types of locations do you look for?

Schneider: Every farm is so different, but when we're going into a place for the first time, we set up locations as we find them. Field corners, fencerows, woods edges – it's so sporadic on most properties, but we set up every good spot we find. And then there are places where you don't really find anything and you have to search for a spot just to put in two sets.

Edges are important, no matter what edge it is. It's becoming popular in agriculture today to have a ditch running through a flat field, sometimes multiple ditches. I check out every one I come across. There can be a million locations to set and you just hit everything that you

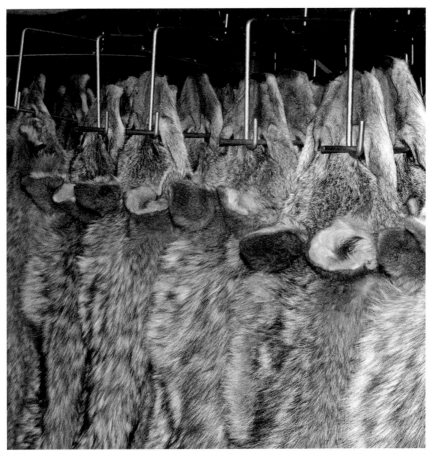

"You can't catch what's not there, and coyote trapping requires a lot of ground."

possibly can, and then you get out of there and move to the next field.

Now, if we're talking the Flint Hills or mountainous areas, we're talking drainages. We basically jump from drainage to drainage and most of them have at least some coyote sign in them. Our first year in an area, we set up every drainage we come to whether we find sign or not. Next year, we'll skip the ones that weren't as productive.

Looking for sign can be very time consuming, especially when you're cold rolling, so if you have plenty of traps, you may as well go ahead and set it up and see what happens. Those traps are better off in the ground than in the back of your truck.

RS: It sounds like you take more of a scatter approach rather than trying to find that one hot spot.

Schneider: Yes, definitely. Let's say we're talking the one square mile theory, and the only thing I have along that one square mile is a fencerow. You have to think about multiple coyotes traveling that area. I know that there's no lure that a coyote will find attractive every time through. Sometimes a lure might not be as effective because of the way we put our sets in.

As a general rule, most "manmade" sets such the dirthole, T-bone set, staked wool set, and staked hide set are what I would call a pup set. For the most part, only a pup is going to work that type of a set. Of the pack of six coyotes working that fencerow, those sets may only work for two of them. So how am I going to get the rest?

Let's say I went down the fencerow and put in two more dirtholes and picked up a third coyote. After that, you can be pretty sure the rest won't be caught in dirthole sets. If that's the only set I know how to make, I'm in big trouble.

It's my viewpoint that it takes no longer to catch the older coyotes than it does the younger coyotes if we put the right set in. So we may put in a dirthole and then move down the fencerow ten paces or more and put in something more subtle, such as a flat set or double mouse hole set.

The double mouse hole set is a trap bedded and blended on the trail the coyotes are traveling, and a hole on one side has a curiosity lure and the hole on the other side has a food lure. The goal is for the coyote to be caught before it even realizes there's a set there. He's trotting down the trail at 3.5 miles per hour and all of a sudden he catches a whiff of lure and stops. To me, that's how you catch all of the coyotes. There's no better place to have a trap than under a pre-existing track. All I have to do is get him to slow down enough to catch him.

I see guys make a scent post by shoving a stick in the ground and putting some gland lure or urine on it. The stick stands out like a sore thumb along the edge of a soybean field. But if they'd just take the time, I'd bet they could find a clump of grass that sticks out and has just as much eye appeal. Whether I find sign there or not, I know that every canine is going to urinate on that clump of grass. All I have to do is

Ed Schneider is one of the top predator trappers in the country.

add a trap and maybe a little bit of gland lure on the crown of the grass. Now, I've made a total ambush type of set that will catch every coyote or bobcat that comes by. The nice thing is, I'm not asking the coyote to do anything. All he has to do is go along with his daily routine.

RS: How important is preseason work?

Schneider: Very important. Get as many dirtholes pre-dug and pre-staked as possible. Instead of putting in 25 sets on day one, that'll allow you to get in 60 sets. All you'll have to do is slap a trap in the ground and go. If you used to average three coyotes out of 25 sets that first check, now you'll average seven.

RS: Fresh dirt has a certain amount of allure to animals. Do you find that pre-digging dirtholes has any negative effects?

Schneider: You're right, which is why, on day one, you're going to take that dull, weathered dirthole and freshen it up again. Add some bait and lure and you'll bring it right back to life. If a coyote has worked that dirthole before, he's lost half of his fear of the set.

One year I had 450 dirtholes dug prior to the season. I caught around 340 coyotes that year. Pre-digging dirtholes gave me the ability to move my line quickly when the time came. I could pull a line one day and set up a whole new one the next, or if I could, that same day.

Richard and I skin an average of 12 coyotes a day, not counting the one to four coyotes we have to throw out every day because they have mange. We move about 30 sets a day, too, but every day we have a catch rate of about 5%. We check a lot of empty sets. But you need to understand that coyotes are not in an area every day, so we set every place we can to average 12.

We've found that if we move our 30 sets today, six of the 12 coyotes we catch tomorrow will come from those new sets. If you go off of that percentage, it gets kind of freaky, doesn't it? You can have sets that have been in the ground six or seven days, but you always need that group of fresh sets to go with them. That's the secret to keeping your catch rates up every day and putting up big numbers.

Visit www.KansasTraplineProducts.com to view Ed Schneider's full line of lures, baits, and trapping supplies.

"To me, a coyote is a coyote, but every bobcat is different. They all have different personalities and appearances."

Lesel Reuwsaat
Strategies for Bobcats

Lesel Reuwsaat's grandparents introduced him to trapping. They were farmers on the East River, South Dakota, who liked to trap during the offseason when they weren't farming. There weren't many coyotes in that region back then, but Lesel still remembers his grandpa talking about the first one he ever caught. Lesel now lives in Western South Dakota and traps full time. He also produces his own line of attractors, Reuwsaat's Extreme Performance Baits and Lures, and has released a number of DVD's that follow him on his personal traplines throughout the West.

RS: In 2011, you left a good job in the corporate world to become a full-time trapper. Where did you work and how did you make that transition?

Reuwsaat: I worked for a company called Dean Foods, which is the largest dairy in the world, and I managed drivers for them. I'd go to work at seven in the morning and get off around four or five in the afternoon, and then go check traps after that until two or three in the morning. In South Dakota, we have a three-day check, so I'd run two different lines, and the third day I'd skin my catch.

The trapping became an addiction and started taking precedence over other things. Eventually, my wife and I went through our budget to see if we could make it work, and here I am, seven years later.

RS: I'm sure fluctuating fur markets blow holes in that budget.

Reuwsaat: Absolutely! When I got out of Dean Foods, the fur market was booming. It couldn't have been a better time. I had two good years of awesome prices on bobcats and coyotes and coons, and then the fur market crashed. Fortunately, that was about the time my bait and lure business started taking off, and it's become a very necessary part of the whole operation.

RS: How did you get started making lures?

Reuwsaat: That was me trying to be thrifty and one thing led to another. I had no mentor to help me formulate lures, I've never bought anybody's recipes, or anything like that. My entire line of baits and lures are 100% my own creation based on my own experiences. I'd run sets in sandy areas, with no trap, so that I could see how the animals responded, and I developed the lures based on the response I got. And I just kept testing them until I got what I wanted.

RS: You've also talked about being thrifty on the trapline as far as catching and utilizing every animal you can. You harvest the fur, collect the glands. All of that is very important for a full-time trapper to do.

Reuwsaat: You have to. In South Dakota, we have a very high-dollar bobcat. If you chased just that bobcat, you'd end up with an atrocious fuel bill because you have to cover so much ground to get to where the 'cats are, unlike Texas where there are bobcats all over the place. In South Dakota, you have to go 50-60 miles to get on target for bobcats.

You also have to keep in mind that, in my best season, I harvested 40 bobcats in South Dakota and 3 in Wyoming. One of those days produced 7 'cats. If you take away the 3 from Wyoming, that means I caught 33 bobcats in South Dakota over the course of a 60-day season. That doesn't pay the bills, unless you're also harvesting the coyotes, 'coons, badgers, skunks, and everything else that goes with it.

The other side of it is that you don't do your ranchers any favors by just targeting the bobcats. But if you help the ranchers and take the coyotes and 'coons out of there, as well, now you have a place to trap year after year.

RS: You started out focusing on bobcats, correct? Why bobcats in

Lesel Reuwsaat with a fine cat in the background.

particular?

Reuwsaat: I did. But the reality of it is that you can go out there and catch 10 coyotes a day, but you might not catch a bobcat every day. The 'cats become a bonus.

Bobcats are very interesting animals. To me, a coyote is a coyote, but every bobcat is different. They all have different personalities and appearances. When I go out and the 'cats aren't hitting, I call it mental warfare. You know what you're doing, and you know you catch them, but you get your butt handed to you for a few checks, and then wham, every check you're hitting them again.

If you go back through your notes, you can usually see where you're going good, and then all of a sudden there's a lull where everything slows down for a period of time. My notes prove it out, and then the switch just turns back on and you're back in business.

RS: Do you think it's weather related or has something to do with animal patterns?

Reuwsaat: I do think it's weather related and also the time of year. For me, there's a time frame in December that you could beat your head against the wall, you know, and then they're moving again and mating season's coming.

RS: In your bobcat trapping DVD, you mention focusing on south-facing slopes in the winter. Tell me more about that and what terrain features you look for.

Reuwsaat: The south-facing slopes melt off first and bobcats will spend more time there. What I envision, too, is that they're sunning themselves on the south-facing slope, and it's warm there in the morning when the sun comes up. You'll notice it in the number of tracks you find, too. They're spending a lot more time on those south-facing slopes than anywhere else.

And then, as far as terrain features go on those slopes, I'm looking for rock ledges, or a spot where the rock ledges break, or where there's a draw. When I'm trapping in Texas, I'm looking for rock outcroppings in the middle of the mesquite. Those are 'cat magnets and I catch them there year after year.

RS: Do you notice any lulls in Texas like you do in South Dakota?

Reuwsaat: In Texas, the slower phase of trapping seems to be when there's no moon. I think that's because your visual attractors aren't as easily seen when it's pitch black out.

RS: You seem to prefer smaller flagging than many 'cat trappers I've seen. In your DVD, you use a lot of little burlap squares as flagging.

Reuwsaat: If you're off location, you need bigger flagging than if you're on location. I'm not trying to pull my 'cats from a long distance because I'm always trying to put my set as close to where they're traveling anyway.

RS: Where do you hang the flagging in relation to the set?

Ralph Scherder • 55

Reuwsaat: I hang my flag between the trap and the dirthole or right over the cubby. I like long sets. I'll make my cubby sets 3 or 4 feet long. This is something that I've really transitioned to over the years. Anything I want to give that 'cat, I want him to have to cross over the trap to get it.

You have to think of a bobcat as having the attention span of a 3-year-old kid. You send a kid to put something in his room and he sees a truck on his way, and so he never makes it to his room. He forgot he was going to put his socks in his drawer. A 'cat is very much the same way. If you flag him away from your set, you're giving him an opportunity to not get caught. So if you're using a flag, hang it so that he has to go passed the trap to get to the flag.

RS: Can you talk more about set construction, such as how wide do you make your cubbies up front?

Reuwsaat: Up front, at the entrance, it's pretty narrow, just wide enough for the levers of the trap. I'm making the bobcat come over the trap to get inside the cubby. When a lot of people talk about cubbies, they're building these monstrosities, these huge forts for the 'cat to go in. You don't need that. My cubbies are literally just a couple of sticks that they can't walk over. It takes five minutes to make. I'm not building little houses in the forest.

RS: I noticed you don't put any sort of a "roof" on your cubbies. They're really just logs arranged in a V-shape with a dirthole in the back of the V.

Reuwsaat: That's a great description of them. They're very simple and quick to make. You want to get sets in the ground. Sets catch 'cats. They don't have to be complicated. And then set the trap out in front of the cubby where they're comfortable. Don't make them come in to get to the trap.

Another thing to think about, too, is that if you do a long cubby, that 'cat has to go in. If you make that same set only 9 to 15 inches deep, he doesn't have to go in to work the cubby. But in a long cubby, if you miss him going in, he has to come out, so you get two chances at him.

RS: Do you also use dirtholes and flat sets?

Reuwsaat: Yes, 90% of what I make are dirthole sets. From Michigan to Texas and everywhere in between, a dirthole will catch coyotes and bobcats.

RS: Do you construct the set differently for 'cats than you would coyotes?

Reuwsaat: For 'cats, the dirthole will be a little bigger and flashier versus just a punch hole for a coyote. I believe in that eye appeal for 'cats. Keep them interested and focused on the sets, and I make those sets backed up against a tree or cedar bush. I also use a lot of blocking to force the 'cat to step on the trap.

RS: How do you lure and bait your dirtholes for 'cats?

Reuwsaat: I use bait down the hole. I use lure on or around the

A fine collection of pelts supporting a good bobcat catch.

dirthole and then give it a shot of urine. And then I'll dip my flag in a long call lure and hang it above the set. I also use rabbit fur or turkey feathers around the set as a visual attractor on the back of the set. It might seem like overkill, but remember, it's like you're dealing with a 3-year-old kid, and you want to give him multiple scents and stimulate multiple senses to keep him focused on the set.

RS: What's your favorite trap for bobcats?

Reuwsaat: I use a boatload of MB-650s. If I'm in areas in Texas where there are lots of gray fox, I drop down to smaller sizes because the MB-650 is just not a good gray fox trap.

RS: I've caught bobcats in #2 coilsprings, but it also seems like I've missed animals that I thought I should've had. Would switching to a bigger trap solve that?

Reuwsaat: When I first started trapping, I used 1.75 coilsprings and definitely had misses, too. If you get a good paw catch on a 'cat, the smaller trap will hold them. Bobcats don't fight the traps the way coyotes do. But going to a bigger trap definitely cuts down on misses because they have such a big paw. I'm a fan of that bigger trap, and it doesn't do any damage to a bobcat's paw.

RS: How do you anchor your bobcat traps?

Reuwsaat: I use either an earth anchor or a drag, never rebar stakes. If you use rebar, you will eventually get to a set and that 'cat won't be there. If you're using a tree as a backing for your set, a 'cat will climb that tree. As it's climbing straight up, it has all the advantage to pull that rebar stake. Absolutely do not use rebar stakes for bobcats.

Ralph Scherder • 57

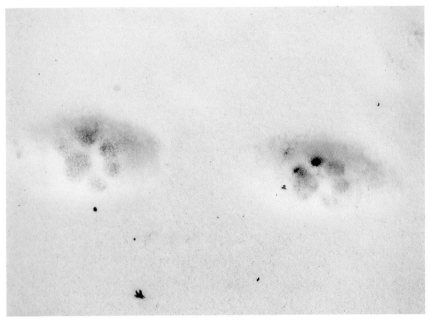

A set of bobcat tracks. Lesel is more selective now and releases many females and younger cats.

RS: Is trapping cats in the west different than trapping them in the south?

Reuwsaat: Yes, very different. At home in South Dakota, we have them condensed down to creeks and rock walls and those types of environments. In Texas, you have miles and miles of greasewood or mesquite or cactus.

The first year I trapped in Texas, the ranch where I stayed wouldn't let me start setting until after hunting season. I was drooling at some of the stuff I had to wait to set because it was rocky, nasty, and the roughest stuff you could imagine. So I set some other areas first and started catching 'cats right away.

When I finally got to set up that rocky area, I caught a bobcat the first night and that was the last 'cat I caught there. It hit me that when you get in that nasty stuff where I was, the rabbit population was squat. Go down in the mesquite bottoms and greasewood, though, and there were jack rabbits everywhere, and that's where the 'cats were. You really have to pay attention to prey species when you're trapping bobcats.

RS: How do your locations change when your setting for bobcats as opposed to setting for coyotes?

Reuwsaat: When I'm setting for coyotes, if I can't hit it with the door of my truck, I'm probably not setting it. You don't need to work any harder than the road to catch coyotes. Bobcats are a little different.

You'll see me walking to catch 'cats. It takes more effort to get into the areas where they like to travel.

You still catch a lot of 'cats in coyote sets. Many people have this misconception that bobcats are strictly sight hunters, but their sense of smell is great, too, and they'll find and work coyote sets. You'd be amazed how many bobcats I release every year from coyote season that were caught before the 'cat season started.

RS: Does releasing them make them harder to catch later?

Reuwsaat: No, I don't think so. I remember one female that I caught five times. She had a gray diamond pattern on her head. I caught her within a two-mile section of creek and released her all five times. Many times I've caught 'cats multiple times.

RS: Do you release females even during the season?

Reuwsaat: It depends upon where I'm trapping. When I first started, I kept everything, and eventually my catch rates went down. So I started releasing females that have been sucked on, which you can tell just by flipping them over if they've been nursing, and I also release the kittens. I'm a lot more selective now.

RS: Any tips for releasing bobcats?

Reuwsaat: Get your catch pole and make sure the cable gets underneath one of the 'cat's front legs and into the armpit and then over the back of the head. That way you can pin them down tight to the ground without worrying about choking them. If you just get around their neck, you have to worry about accidentally choking them. I don't want to have to turn in a bobcat that was caught out of season. To kill that resource and not be able to use it would just be terrible.

To view Lesel Reuwsaat's full line of trapping scents, visit www. ReuwsaatBaitandLure.com.

"I can catch almost any animal out there, but it's the ones that are shy to the trap that really tune me up."

Rusty Johnson
Down to the Last One

Rusty Johnson of Chula, Georgia, has been trapping for 40 years, the last 13 of which have been spent as a professional trapper. His interest in trapping began when he was 12. Nobody in his family had ever trapped before, so he educated himself by reading books and magazines such as Fur-Fish-Game. Since those early beginnings, Rusty has trapped in nine states and through years of research and experimentation has developed his own line of attractors known as Country Boy Lures. He has served as an instructor at Mark June's Predator Trapping Academy.

RS: What were you early trapline experiences like?

Johnson: I basically started by catching raccoons my first year, in 1977. There weren't a lot of trappers who wanted to share information back then. There were books and magazines, but no videos. The second year, when I was 13, I started trapping predators and caught a few bobcats and gray fox as well as my first coyote. After that, I got the trapping bug and just couldn't turn it loose.

I graduated high school and went to work in a factory and trapped on the side. Fur was valuable then. I got $18-24 for 'coons sold green, $40-50 for red fox, $20 for coyotes, which nobody really targeted back then, and around $90 for bobcats.

RS: What made you want to be a trapper and learn more about trapping?

Johnson: I'm a true sportsman. I love to hunt, fish, and trap, and if I'm not doing it, I'm thinking about it. That's basically my life. Trapping tied right in with the hunting. We didn't have a lot of deer back then, and you had to hunt hard to kill one. You had to learn about the animals, which is what you have to do with trapping, too. Each animal has a pattern, and if you want to be successful at it, you'll learn as much as you can about each one. When I first started trapping, I didn't even know how to put up fur until a gentleman up the road taught me how to skin 'coon. I just really wanted to catch the animals.

RS: When was that moment when everything clicked for you as a trapper?

Johnson: That's been an ongoing process. I can catch almost any animal out there, but it's the ones that are shy to the trap that really tune me up. I'm fascinated by the one that's giving me a hard time.

The last 13 years, I've been full-time trapping, traveling the country doing predator control work, mostly for coyotes. You have to be knowledgeable of coyotes in order to catch what I consider the last one.

That's always my goal, to catch the last one.

The last dairy farm I trapped was three years ago. They lost 36 calves in one year, 12 the next year, and now the last couple of years they haven't lost any. It was a 900-acre dairy farm and I caught close to 20 coyotes in two-and-a-half years.

RS: That's not as many coyotes as I'd expect considering all the calves that were killed.

Johnson: Once a coyote learns how to kill a calf or a deer, they're experts at it. That's when they give you problems. But not every coyote's a killer.

When you go on a job and someone tells you they have problems with coyotes, they tell you they have hundreds of them. Most times it's not that many. For instance, if it's 1,000 acres, you're probably not going to have 40-50 coyotes, in most places. Only in certain places, like Texas or Kansas, are numbers that high. In most states, you can't expect that.

RS: When you first arrive on a job and the landowner tells you what's happening, what's your first step? Are you very selective when choosing set sites or do you just try to get as many traps out as possible and cover every travelway you can?

Johnson: The first thing I do is use a GPS to track the perimeter so that I can isolate the area and know the region that I have to work with. I only set the pinch-points first and then fill in every day on sign. I look for water, too. All the animals, at some point, will be coming to the water.

In some areas, the ground is hard and it's difficult to find sign, so you have to really study it to find tracks and scat. Like Tom Krause says, though, if you've got a hunch about a spot, you just have to set it. If you're going into that circle every day, then you've got a good concept of where to set the traps.

I don't want to spook them, which is why I don't set a lot of traps the first day. It's the same with baits and lures. Always hold something back. Don't show your hand the first few days. Try to keep something that will help you get that hard-to-catch coyote later on. It's easy to catch the cream of the crop those first few days, but those last ones can be tough.

I use pretty much the same sets everywhere I go. My main set is the dirthole, and then, on the back end of the trapline, I start making more flat sets to catch the hard coyotes.

RS: If you're trapping a place for a couple of weeks, do you notice your presence having any effect on how coyotes travel or use the property?

Johnson: Yes, coyotes will start avoiding where you've been traveling. At that point, you look for places off the beaten trail. You might have to walk a bit to find those places that are kind of quiet and there's no activity. They'll lay up in those areas. That's where you can really go in and get the last few.

RS: Let's say you're running the 'line and you come across a random

Rusty Johnson with a nice coyote double.

track where you hadn't seen any before. Do you set up on it or are you looking for locations with more concentrated sign?

Johnson: If it wasn't there the day before, yes. The good trappers who are getting paid to clean out a place are reading sign every day and filling in as they go.

Once I set a trap, I'm doing it with confidence that I'll catch something there. Once I make a catch, I reset the trap on the outside of that catch circle because some coyotes won't work a set where another has been caught. Not all of them, but some of them, and I'm there to catch that last one, so I can't afford to wait until he comes around again to find out how he'll react to the catch circle. So I'll either leave that one in the catch circle and set a fresh trap or pull and reset the same one outside the catch circle.

RS: How hard is it to catch that last one sometimes?

Johnson: Sometimes it's impossible, but there are places where I've felt like I cleaned them out.

I trapped and collared coyotes for a University of Georgia study and they found that coyotes in Georgia, Alabama, and South Carolina have a home range of 6-8 square miles, and that's based on a lot of coyotes. During that study, in six days in Alabama we caught three coyotes twice, and they were all adults.

RS: That's interesting because I've heard some guys say if a coyote is released or pulls out of a trap that you'll never catch it again.

Johnson: They say the same thing even if a coyote just snapped the trap. But I believe you can catch educated coyotes, just like I believe you

Most of Rusty's predator control work is for coyotes.

can educate coyotes. Sometimes you can educate them even if they don't work your set. If you use the same lures and baits at every set, or if you make your sets the same way every time, coyotes will pattern you. It's happened to me before.

Let's say a group of coyotes passes through and you catch a couple of them. The ones you didn't catch are pretty good at patterning that smell and that look, so you have to change it up if you want to get them, too. Having coyotes pattern you or your sets will educate them quicker than having a trap snapped in their faces.

If a coyote walked right down the middle of the road without checking either of my sets, I have to figure out what's going on. A lot of times it's the wind direction. But if the wind is right and the set is right, and the coyote still didn't work the set, then there's something else going on.

RS: So you've had that, too, where animals sometimes just walk by sets? Many trappers don't realize that even the professionals have the same troubles at times.

Johnson: We all do, believe me. You learn from your mistakes. Every experience can teach you something. Coyotes will adapt to anything, and sometimes you have to adapt your techniques to fit the situation.

RS: When you're on a job, what do you do about a coyote that's "uncatchable?"

Johnson: If they're coming through every two or three days, you can usually figure them out. The hardest coyote to catch is the one that only passes through once a week. You can only try your best.

I had one coyote that I tried to blind set on the dairy farm I told you about. He came through a little wash and I saw where he crossed the road. I set a trap in that wash in a gap that was barely wide enough to fit my MB-550. It rained that night and the coyote crossed the road. He stopped before the wash and went up the bank about 15 feet away from my set. I had no bait or lure on that set, and I made it in about two minutes and was in and out, yet he still avoided it.

Two days later, it rained again. Once again, this coyote came out onto the road and avoided the wash and went up the bank. I told the rancher than I couldn't catch it right now and needed to give it a break.

That coyote had already killed two calves, about $2,000 worth. About a month later, the rancher called me and said the coyote had killed two more calves, so I went back down there the next day and I sprayed myself and my equipment with scent eliminator.

There was a dirt road around this 900-acre dairy farm and I could tell there was only one track coming in and going out over two or three days. I went up the road and found a trail where he'd crossed, then I circled around and came to the trail from back side and found a good spot. I set a trap and left immediately, backing out the same way I'd come, and the next day I had the coyote. That was the first selfie I ever took with a phone. I was proud.

Once a coyote learns how to kill a cow or calf, they're experts at it, and that's when they give you problems. Not every coyote is a killer.

RS: In your brochure for Country Boy Lures, you mention that some trappers claim that all lures and baits work, but you found that some work better than others. What is the proper way to test a lure or bait?

Johnson: I test my lures by picking out the best spot and making two sets 8 to 10 feet apart. You can't make them on different sides of the road and put a lure in the first set and then the one you want to test in the second. They have to be on the same side and they both have to be in the sweet spot. And then keep notes about how the animals react. Let the notes tell you which one's working better.

I think all baits and lures will work. At some point, they'll catch a coyote. I think of it this way – you can set right beside the road and catch a coyote the first night, or you can set 20 feet away and eventually catch a coyote. Kind of the same concept with lures and baits. I try to go with the better averages rather than just what will catch one, and the only way to figure that out is by keeping notes.

RS: Any advice for new trappers?

Johnson: I'd tell them to buy good equipment, read books, watch videos, and put your heart into it and learn as much as you can about it. Having a partner can help, too, if you have the same work ethic. A partner can keep you going if you have a bad day.

The best thing you can have in your back pocket is confidence, but not so much confidence that you can't learn anything. Trapping is a life journey. Don't ever get to the point where you think you can't learn anymore. That coyote will humble all of us sooner or later, and there's nothing you can do about it.

Trappers new to the sport have a great advantage over trappers years ago because of the wealth of knowledge that's out there. Many of them want to catch coyotes before they ever learn to catch raccoons.

I had a feller tell me a long time ago that you're not a trapper until you know how to put up your own fur. You have to know how to handle the fur and have respect for the animals that we catch, and there's a lot of truth to that. It all makes you a trapper.

To learn more about Country Boy Lures, visit www. RustyJohnsonPredatorLures.com.

Jeff Dunnier is a well-known fixture at trapping conventions.

Jeff Dunnier
The Beaver Business

Originally from Ohio, Jeff Dunnier moved to Marshall, Texas, with his wife Jill in 1982 to trap beaver. For the next 11 years, Dunnier trapped for the army on an 8,500-acre reservation and for many northeast Texas landowners while also working a regular full-time job. In 1993, Dunnier quit that job to pursue his own nuisance control business. His first year, he racked up 50,000 miles, 1,000 beaver, and 115 otter over three states trapping for timber companies. He is the author of the book, Beaver Business.

RS: Who got you interested in trapping?

Dunnier: I picked it up on my own in 1964. I've always been crazy about animals, like most trappers, and I'd always bring stuff home. One time, I had a praying mantis cocoon in a jar with holes in it, and all of a sudden, all these baby praying mantises were showing up in my underwear. My mom asked if I had any more of those cocoons, and I said yeah, there's a bunch of them on the heater in the laundry room. We had praying mantises everywhere!

I've always had a passion for wildlife and nature. My first traps were set in '64 and my first catch was a skunk, which I thought was a mink. It was up in a den and I pulled it out. Of course, it sprayed all over my brand new school clothes, so my parents made me quit. But in 1971, I started trapping again and haven't stopped since.

RS: What did you mostly target at first?

Dunnier: At first, it was a combination. I wanted to catch fox. We didn't have many coyotes at that time. I liked my water trapping, too. We didn't have any beavers where I was in Montgomery County, but they had some in southern Ohio, and I went down there once.

I started trapping beaver in excess when I was stationed at Fort Campbell, right on the border of Kentucky and Tennessee.

RS: Is there a difference between trapping for fur versus damage control?

Dunnier: There's a big difference. For one, the habits of the animals change in the summertime because of the heat. They don't feed as much. Beaver, for instance, won't move a lot in the dead of summer unless you're getting a lot of rain. When you get a lot of rain, they move up out of the river bottoms into higher ground, ponds and lakes. I run into a lot of people who trap for fur and would like to also do nuisance control. I always recommend they try it first before jumping in full time because their habits are different and it takes a different approach.

RS: They can't just skim the cream and move on, either. Most jobs probably expect you to get all of them right down to the last one.

Dunnier: Exactly. There's no leaving any seed on beavers.

In my area, and all through the south, we've got so many beavers. It seems like every time it rains, it's raining beavers. I work on the mine lakes on the reclaims. We've got the Sabine River on one side of us, and then a bunch of huge lakes with tributaries that connect into a lot of our run-off water from the mines, so we've always got beaver. It's never ending.

I do a lot for timber companies, also. And for some reason, a lot of your timber land is bottom land. In the early 1980s, they started managing their bottom land and a lot of people were doing nuisance control in the south. You still have some of them, but many of the big companies have sold out and broken up into smaller companies and they don't do as much damage control as they used to.

RS: What are some of the biggest challenges you face as a damage control trapper?

Dunnier: I would say the heat of the summer, the mosquitos and moccasins and anything that sting or bite you. When I first started, I was removing bats, raccoons, and stuff up in the attics. Now, going up into culverts that beaver have dammed up can be an adventure. Most of them that have a trickle of water in them, and even if they don't, they have those soft limbs that move around and you learn to let go of those real quick. In all the years that I've cleaned culverts, I've never been bitten, thank God, but I've come pretty close.

RS: How did you develop your panel system for trapping beaver and otter?

Dunnier: It started with the way a lot of beaver trappers use sticks to narrow down runways or entrances to culverts so that they can put in a 330. Sometimes you have to use a lot of sticks as fencing to force the animal through the trap. Instead of doing all that, I started using sixteen-foot hog panel fence cut into sections. I wire six panels to a bundle, which makes it easy to carry them to the control spot. The control spot is the dam or culvert where you can manipulate the water by creating a hole in the dam that will cause the beavers to come to you.

I then use 330 or 280 bodygrips with tall supports. The object is to use the panels to narrow down the travel ways the beaver are using, then set your traps in the runways between the panels. It's much quicker and easier than spending time shoving sticks in the mud.

RS: Beavers are very industrious animals.

Dunnier: They're very strong, too. I've always been amazed at the size and weight of some of the things they've used to build their dams. I've seen them use 10-pound boulders to anchor their dams, or they'll float huge logs to use. They're a hard-working animal.

I've been blasting dams since the early 90s. Some require more dynamite because of what's in them, the consistency of the mud and how well it's packed. If there's not much mud or sand, you don't get a good blow, but you do if it's packed down good. Having a blasting license is a big plus if you're doing damage control in the south.

RS: If you totally remove a dam, will they rebuild it?

Dunnier: In my experience, they always seem to come back and rebuild in the same spot. And it can happen pretty fast. I've blown dams and had the water stopped up again already the next morning.

That's where my panel system really comes into play, too. Once I blast a hole in the dam, I can now control the water flow. I set up the panels with the 330s and let the beavers come to me.

Jeff has developed the panel system for setting for beaver. The panels are generally quicker and more versatile than using on-location sticks.

I don't even bother with the houses anymore. I feel like the more you mess with the houses, the more it makes the beavers insecure and on the lookout for danger, and they might not function in a normal fashion after that. But if they got a break in the dam, they know it, and they know they've got to go fix it. They're not thinking about danger. They're just thinking about fixing the dam.

RS: In your book, Beaver Business, you mention that you've kept records on the wildlife you've trapped for 30 years, particularly the beaver. Why do you find beavers so fascinating?

Dunnier: I just wanted to know as much about them as I could. Over the years, by keeping records, I've found that some of the things you read about beavers aren't quite so. I kept track of their weights, how many kits they have, different locations and what I caught them in. I've kept a lot of records of otter, too. In fact, I've got more data on otter down in Austin than probably anybody. Lengths, weights, number of offspring, what county they came from, stuff like that.

RS: What's something you've learned to be different than many people think?

Dunnier: Litter size would be one. Out of two female beavers that were in the 60-65-pound range, one had six offspring and another had seven offspring. I really think the habitat determines how many offspring the female has. Age also has an effect. If a female is a first-time breeder, she'll most likely have one to three kits. As the female gets older, and the habitat is well-established, her body gets bigger and she's capable of having larger litters. But if you take that same female beaver, say a 60-pounder, and put her into a smaller habitat, such as a creek, she might have only one or two kits instead of six or seven in the larger habitat.

Down here in the south, normally a beaver will have one litter per year. But I've found where two different females have been bred twice in the same year, probably because they had litters very early in the spring and it was an El Nino year.

When I open the breeding females, you can tell how many offspring they've had by the number of sacks present or will have by the number of actual kits present. But there will also be black spots on the fallopian tubes, and counting them will tell you how many offspring she had.

RS: If you're going into a job and catch that big female first, could you then estimate how many others still occupy the area?

Dunnier: Yes, as long as you know the history of the pond. If there haven't been any trappers there in the past three years, or if nobody has shot and killed any, you should know about how many you're dealing with.

A lot of people don't think about that, but it's important when you're nuisance trapping. If you can catch the big female, she pretty much tells the tale right there. Of course, in habitats where there's more than one colony, that's all thrown out the window.

RS: What's the best way to use beaver lure?

Dunnier: There are several ways I've used it. I always liked Charlie Dobbins and copied his sets. You can take two or three poles and drive them in the ground to make a teepee, then hang your snare below in the water and put the lure up above on the poles. Sometimes I do put lure in conjunction with my panel system. I place it inside of the cage that surrounds the dam or culvert to entice the beaver to go into the 330s.

RS: I think it's interesting that beavers are one of the only animals that changes their environment to suit their needs. Sometimes they get the reputation for being no harder to catch than a big muskrat. How true or false is that? Do they have the potential to become educated and hard to catch?

Dunnier: I feel like they can associate things such as danger with a smell and start avoiding certain situations. But with my panel system, if you have the access to a control spot where you can manipulate the water to bring the beavers to you, it makes them a lot easier. The quicker you can take them out, the less chance they have to become cautious. I've taken whole colonies out in one night.

RS: Have you ever had that one beaver that you just could not catch?

Dunnier: I have. In fact, I have one place where I've taken a lot of beaver, but there are always more moving in by following a stream up to the pond. For some reason, which I haven't been able to figure out, this one pond will either give me a bunch of trouble and I can't get them out, or the new ones will come in and I'll take those out right away.

But, say I've caught two or three and they're still building up, but I'm not catching any more. That's when I try other types of sets. I'll start using snares and footholds. I never start out using lure at all with my panel system because beavers losing their water is what's going to attract them to your traps anyway. Always save your lure as your last resolve, the last trick in the bag.

Certain times of the year, beaver respond better to lures. During breeding season in the spring, for instance, or during the fall shuffle. The reason is because you've added something that they're not used to, and they want to find out more about that other beaver that's move into their area.

When I take the castors and oil sacs out of a beaver, if I press down on the castor and there's a lot of urine mixed with castor coming out, I'll collect it into a bottle. I'll milk it out so I can use it at another set where maybe I'm having problems with other beavers. Using urine and castor off another beaver seems to work really well for those ones that are really hard to catch.

Jeff with a nice catch of otter.

"I've caught a lot of coons on red meat baits, but a loud fish bait really cuts through the night air. And actually, if somebody pinned me in the corner and made me pick just one bait to use for everything when dryland trapping, I'd go with fish bait, even for the canines."

Scott Welch
Trapping Masked Bandits

S cott Welch says there are certain things that appeal to you in life and you can't always explain it. That's what trapping was like for him, at least. As a boy, he spent hours in his grandparents' basement reading articles by E.J. Dailey and Bill Nelson in old issues of Fur-Fish-Game and the trapping fire was lit. Over the years, Scott has developed his own line of trapping scents, Welch's High Production Lures and Baits, as well as took over the late Carroll "Blackie" Black's line of lures, Blackie's Blend.

RS: When did you get involved in trapping?

Welch: I was young. My biological father was killed in an accident before I was born. My grandparents on my father's side lived just up the road from us. My grandpa was older and already retired, so he let me hang around. He hunted groundhogs and fished all summer and hunted deer and called fox later on. Anything you could do outdoors, he did it, so I was exposed to all of that very early on. My grandpa wasn't much of

Scott Welch with a a fine day's catch of raccoon. "You keep working at it and it'll pay off for you."

a teacher, but he always gave you an opportunity to learn. Maybe that's what a good teacher is, after all.

My grandpa was always pretty tight-fisted and never bought trapping lure or bait or even fishing bait. You either found it or made it yourself. We chopped up groundhogs to use as bait and made fish oil, so almost from the time I started trapping, I started messing around with making lures and baits as well.

RS: At what point did you meet and befriend Blackie?

Welch: I was around 11 or 12 years old. My mom was the postmaster of the little town of Nashville, Ohio, not far from where Blackie lived. That's where they sent all their catalogues out of. Mom got to be friends with them just from seeing them every day and brought home a catalogue and I looked through that thing over and over again. Finally, she asked if she could bring me over to see him. At that time, he was still making his lures and baits out of an old township house and they'd refurbished it for his lure and bait making. That would've been around 1986 or so. He was fairly young in the business when I first met him.

RS: Did you ever get the chance to trap with Blackie?

Welch: I didn't. I took instruction from him for a couple things but it was always during the offseason. I'd asked him about taking instruction on his actual trapline but he was so old school and secretive. He'd tell me, "You live too close to me to teach you everything I know." I could always weasel a little out of him but he drew the line there.

I came into trapping right at the tail end of the fur boom, and my trapping partner Mike Taylor and I averaged $34 or $36 for our raccoons, which my grandpa helped us put up. You could buy a new dozen of Montgomery 1.5 coils for $35. So I swapped a few coon for a few dozen traps and still walked out of there with a few hundred bucks in my pocket and I thought, holy cow, a guy could make a living doing this. That kinda ruined me right from the start.

Raccoon trapping got a hold of me at an early age, and being around Blackie just added to it.

RS: What do you look for in a raccoon trapping location?

Welch: Everybody laughs at me for the video I did called *Raccoons and Cornfields,* but where I live, that's pretty much it. If you have corn, creeks, and standing timber, you're always going to have raccoons.

Like a lot of other things, once you know what you're looking for, you can buzz by a lot of unpromising spots to get to the good ones. My wife laughs when we're driving along and I can look down the road and say, "I'll bet there's a coon trail right down here," and once we get closer, nine times out of ten, sure enough there's a coon trail crossing the road.

Deer hunting guru and writer Gene Wentzel probably described it the best. I heard him use a phrase once about reading deer sign. He said it's like telling the difference between a woman's handwriting and a man's handwriting. You learn it from experience and you can't always explain it, but you know the difference as soon as you see it.

Good trapping locations, whether for fox, coyote, or raccoons, get to be the same way. It's a long process that stems from success as well as lack of success and then putting it all together so that you recognize it at a glance. You don't even have to think about it.

RS: What specific features are you looking for? What aspects combine to create a great location?

Welch: I always like where a drainage starts. A waterway. Maybe even just a wet spot in the field where they let the grass grow up. That'll trickle down, catch a little branch, and there's always water there. Many times, those places will come out to a point and they'll have that good, mature timber on the edge of a field. Any time you're seeing places like that, where those drainages starts or ends, you'll always have coon there. Those are the types of places I'm talking about being able to find those heavy coon trails. You don't even have to have the cornfields present. They'll use those places as travel routes to other food sources, too.

During the late season, look for those hardwood ridges and rock faces where big boar coon like to run when they're searching for females. That's where it pays to know your area because a lot of these winter locations will be situational. It's important to remember, though, that

Living close to Blackie (left) and meeting him when a youngster gave Scott Welch (right) further incentive to trap raccoon. Scott developed his own Welch's High Production Lures and Baits, then bought the Blackie's Blend line to add to it.

you're not going to catch the same numbers of coon like you will earlier in the season.

RS: Raccoons have the reputation of being easy to trap, but sometimes they can be extremely difficult, especially when you get one of those big old wise boars. I've always thought that a big old boar coon is one of the hardest buggers to catch.

Welch: Absolutely. Any big, mature animal of any species tends to have its own routine and doesn't hang around with the rest of the pack. For instance, here in Ohio, I snare a lot of raccoons. You see those trails that are packed down in the mud and it seems like a thousand coon are traveling them. Once in awhile you'll catch a big boar in them, but usually those are mama coons and young-of-the-year coons. But when you get those real subtle trails coming off of a ridgeline, or coming out of the hardwoods where they're moving into a cornfield, and they're not those packed down trails, those are where you catch the big adult boar coons. Those coons that have their ears rubbed down to little nubs, they're the ones you want. They're hard to get in those packed down mud trails the others use.

Sometimes in the late season, I'll get out there in the cold and set for coon. You don't need a big weather swing. That's something Blackie taught me a long time ago. It can be five degrees every night for a week and then warm up to 20 or 25 degrees, and it's still cold, but it's enough of a temperature swing to get those boar coons moving.

I remember Blackie talking about using a spud bar to bust ice off the shelves along the river bank because he knew the coon were going to be moving. And it's the same whether you're running along the water or if you're snaring or using dog-proof traps during that late season when you're going to catch those boar coon, even a little bit of a weather front can get them out of their dens.

RS: Later in the season, January and February, sometimes it can be hard to get a raccoon to slow down long enough to work a set.

Welch: I've always had luck late in the season using a loud gland lure. Actually, coyote gland lure is really good on late season coons. I can't explain why but it definitely works.

When you're trying to get them to slow down, like you said, I use a lot of fish meal and just throw handfuls of it around to get that odor volume up around the set. Also, that time of year, a catch circle really helps with lots of eye appeal and nose appeal. In that late season, you don't want to be too subtle or too cute with your sets. You want to really grab that coon's attention.

RS: What types of sets do you like to use?

Welch: Anymore, like most guys, I use a lot of dog-proof traps because they're so easy to plug in. For late season coons, dirtholes and even flat sets are great, and you can even make it look like a catch circle when you make those sets. Eye appeal is huge for coon.

"It can be five degrees every night for a week and then warm up to 20 or 25 degrees, and it's still cold, but it's enough of a temperature swing to get those boar coons moving."

RS: Preferred baits?

Welch: I've caught a lot of coons on red meat baits, but a loud fish bait really cuts through the night air. And actually, if somebody pinned me in the corner and made me pick just one bait to use for everything when dryland trapping, I'd go with fish bait, even for the canines.

RS: You mentioned that you trap a lot of cornfields. How do you compete with that food source and get the coons to stop and work the set?

Welch: That can be tricky. That's where snaring really shines. Probably 75% of the coon I catch in cornfields are blind-caught in snares. Even if I'm using dirtholes or dog-proof traps, I don't try to get too cute with them. I slap those suckers in right on the trail or next to the trail where coons can't miss them.

Those first 10-12 days of the season when coons are really plowing into the food sources, you gotta put that set where they're going to run their noses right into it. Coons are very lazy animals. They're going to climb out of the den and hit that trail right to the food source. That's why those trails are there, from traveling the same route back and forth every night.

RS: How many snares do you set on a trail?

Welch: Depends on the location. I had a location where a waterway came up into a cornfield and I hung eight snares in that one, 24-foot by 24-foot area. The next day I caught seven coons there. When you have to reload your revolver at one stop, that's a pretty good location!

During those first 10-12 days of the season, you really have to make hay. You may only get two, three, four nights when those coons are really moving and you've gotta take advantage of that, which is a good reason to set heavy. Now, catching seven in one spot doesn't happen that often. You have to have the right conditions, numbers of coons, and the right weather, but when all of those line up, you have to be in position to take advantage of it. I always say you're going to catch 80% of your coon on 20% of your checks.

RS: How do you limit body catches when snaring coon and get a higher percentage of neck catches?

Welch: First of all, if you're not loading your snares, you're going

"Raccoon trapping got a hold of me at an early age, and being around Blackie just added to it."

to have a hard time catching them by the neck. When it's not loaded, you get that teardrop shape and leave coons an awful lot of room to get their front legs through the loop and it's not going to close fast enough. A loaded snare is rounder and fires faster.

The other thing is, guys would be shocked to know how small you can make the loop for coon. I make the loop five to six inches and set it four and a half to five and a half inches off the ground. You want the loop to hit right under his chin and fire. I'd say three quarters of the coon I catch are either by the neck or around the neck and one front leg, which is also a good catch that doesn't cause much fur damage. Coons are rascals, though. Even with loading the snares and using small loops, they'll find their way through it now and then, but rarely passed their armpits.

RS: What sort of preseason work do you do?

Welch: I build new snares. I do like to go out two or three days ahead of time and see where the cornfields are and which ones have been harvested. I'll also mark trap locations with surveyor's tape so that on set day I can jump from ribbon to ribbon instead of wasting time figuring out where to hang the snare. That helps you get an extra 40 or 50 sets out that day when you know you have a good night coming. That adds up quick.

When Blackie trapped the rivers, he had pockets dug and drowning rigs already set up. All of that saves time. In regards to pre-baiting, I don't know if it helps the coon catch much. If there are coon in the area, and you're on location, you're going to catch him that first night just as well with a new set as with one you made a week ahead of time, although it might save you a little bit of time to have it made ahead of time.

RS: How does the corn harvest effect your game plan?

Welch: You have a little bit of a window there between the corn harvest and when the coon catch will fall off. If it's within five days or so, I'm not too concerned. Long, dry summers and an early harvest are a bigger deal. Farmers get bored and, at least around here, they'll bush hog those cornstalks down, and that makes it difficult to catch coons. Really, you want the weather that farmers hate. Wet weather keeps farmers out of the fields and coons make a lot of trails.

RS: So if there's an early harvest, do you focus more on waterways?

Welch: Exactly right. You just regroup and do what you need to do to keep catching fur. It's hard to get those big number nights, but it's not like those coons disappear. They're there somewhere. You just have to hustle around to find them and cover more area and keep working at it. That's how it is with pretty much everything. You keep working at it and it'll pay off for you.

"Every little thing you do adds to your success. Using a bigger trap might add 1%. Using dogs on the trapline might add another 2%. None of these are earth-changing things, but they add up."

Mark Zagger
A Coyote Education

Mark Zagger of Syracuse, NY, makes catching coyotes look easy. In an area where 30 coyotes a year is a big deal, Zagger often harvests over a hundred. In fact, he's averaged 130 coyotes per year over the past decade, and he's done it while trapping only three weeks per season! Zagger has trapped in seven different states and shares his coyote knowledge with others through his trapping school, Coyote U, which he offers twice per year, along with demos at conventions and the occasional magazine article.

RS: How has coyote trapping shaped your life?

Zagger: It might sound corny, but a lot of the success I've had in life can be traced back to my love of trapping coyotes. The gentleman that hired me to work for Pyramid Network Services, where I'm now a partner and Vice President, first heard about me back in the early 1990s because I was one of the few guys around who could trap coyotes. He had a 1,200-acre farm that he bowhunted and managed for whitetails. He asked me if I'd be willing to help him with the coyotes on his property. I trapped on his farm for 4 or 5 years and he was so happy with the numbers I was trapping annually.

He worked in Atlanta, Georgia, where the company was headquartered, and wanted to buy some tanned coyotes off of me from New York. I told him I'd meet him at the farm one day. I pulled in and I was wearing a suit and tie on my way to work as an account executive at Federal Express, and I had my Chevy Lumina, the ultimate sales vehicle at that time! He said, 'Where are you going, a funeral or something?' I said I was working. In all the time I'd known him, we'd never talked about work until then. At that time, his company was just starting to boom, and he was surrounding himself with people he knew and liked. He asked if I knew anything about telecommunications, which I didn't. He said his company was growing and he was looking for new talent. We started talking about it, and in 1999, I went to work for him at the lowest of levels, but that put me on a career path that was unachievable where I had been working. And all because I was good at catching coyotes.

RS: What was the first animal you ever trapped?

Zagger: In 1976, I caught my first muskrat. It was in a little trickle that I put a Conibear in and eventually caught a muskrat. I'll never forget it. I sold it for $9.50, which seemed like a million dollars to me at the time. That would be like a $50 muskrat now, or more!

I always wanted to be a canine trapper. I read all the trapping magazines, even back when Tom Krause was the editor of The Trapper,

Mark Zagger with what in most circles is considered to be a pile of coyotes!

it was the canines that intrigued me. I struggle to tell you my wife Gina's birthday or our wedding anniversary, but on October 21, 1978, I caught my first red fox. It was the first check of the season. It felt good and I imagined writing books and making videos, but what's funny is that I didn't catch another fox for two years. That's how bad I was. I realized I had to go get some teaching from other people. Over the years, I've taken lessons from Ray Milligan, Craig O'Gorman, Ron and Pete Leggett, Johnny Thorpe, and others.

RS: What were some of the mistakes you made when trying to catch more fox?

Zagger: I worried way too much about human odor. I dyed and waxed everything from my traps to my bike to my friends to cut down on odor. Say I was walking down a farm lane and veered off to make a dirthole set. I would spray the entire path where I walked up to the set with fox urine trying to mask my scent. I gave red fox way too much credit. I thought they were super human. If you were to follow me around now, I don't even talk about human odor. I tell people not to worry about it. It's not really even on my radar.

I think canine trapping is more location driven. If you see a beaten down raccoon trail, a muddy muskrat run, or a beaver run, you can set a Conibear and you get them. Canine locations aren't quite as obvious to new trappers. But I'd be willing to bet that, if I put my nose to the ground back when I first started, I'd find the tracks and turds that I do now and picked better locations.

RS: You're originally from Cortland, Ohio. In the late 1980s, you moved from Altoona, Pennsylvania, to Syracuse, New York. What was it like transitioning from trapping fox to trapping coyotes?

Zagger: In 1989, my first year in New York, I caught 14 coyotes. I was using 1.75 coilsprings, and if I caught 14, I lost 14. This was way before bigger traps became so popular. I remember buying my first #2 Northwoods, which are similar to a #2 Bridger, and I'd only set them in the winter in the snow because I thought they were HUGE! Hand me that same trap now and I look at it like it's a muskrat trap. And it's not about holding the coyote as much as it's about coming up through snow, ice, or mud. Bigger is better.

RS: What's your favorite trap now?

Zagger: I'm a Jake guy. I use J.C. Conner's Jake Trap pretty much exclusively. I've built my whole system around that trap, from the way I make my dirtholes to the way I build my Pipe Dream Set. It's the only trap on the markret that's truly a square jaw. That doesn't mean anything other than it's easier for me to dig a square bed and bed that trap the way I like to do it.

I have used every trap on the market. As I switched from 1.75s to #2s to #3s and built my arsenal, I was that typical guy who'd buy six traps from one place, 20 from another, and then two dozen more from somewhere else. You'd look at my bin of 100 traps and find 10 different models. Later, when I started buying bigger traps, I was also paying someone else to modify them to what I wanted. When it was all said and done, the traps with modifications were costing me almost as much as the higher quality traps that were good to go right out of the box.

If you're going to make a set and find yourself reaching past certain traps in your bin to get to the traps you prefer using, then those other traps probably shouldn't be in there. As time went on, I found myself more often reaching past all the others and grabbing a Jake Trap.

Every little thing you do adds to your success. Using a bigger trap might add 1%. Using dogs on the trapline might add another 2%. None of these are earth-changing things, but they add up.

I tell guys all the time to streamline their equipment. I know Gerald Schmitt does it with mink trapping. Every trap is the same. They have the same length of chain, same modifications, same swivels on the end. It gets you into a system and a rhythm. When I kneel down to make a Pipe Dream Set, every set is identical because I'm going to put that Jake Trap in there every time. It speeds things up and makes me a more efficient trapper. It might add only 5 coyotes to my total at the end of the year, but that's 5 I wouldn't have had.

RS: You mentioned using dogs on the trapline. How long have you been doing that and what have dogs taught you?

Zagger: Guys have been doing that out west for a century or more.

A good friend of mine who moved from New York to Montana was an O'Gorman protégé, and I rode out there with him in the late-90s and he introduced me to using dogs on the trapline. It was an eye opener.

What the dogs taught me most goes back to what I was saying about reading sign. You go to a new farm and get out of the truck. There's five different locations and they all look pretty good, so you set them up. I'll pull in with my dogs and cast them out of the truck and let them go. Rusty and Boone, those were their names, they'd find coyote turds, fox turds, and, more importantly, the grass tufts that canines were already marking. It took the guesswork out of finding locations. Those dogs finding sign gave me all the confidence in the world. They took me from a "location" trapper to a trapper setting up on sign.

Another thing the dogs taught me was this. Every book tells you to make a scent post set by finding a stick three inches in diameter, pounding it into the ground at a 45-degree angle, and then bedding your trap at the base of it. Guess what? Those don't exist in farm country because the farmers knock them down with their equipment when they're working their fields. Where I trap, it's those dark clumps of grass that stick out like a sore thumb in the fields that attract canines. When my dogs found those tufts, I could tell by their body language that they were being marked by coyotes. I'd set them, sometimes doctor them up with a shot of gland lure or urine and catch coyotes there. Sometimes I just set the trap and don't add any lure at all and still get coyotes.

I use that grass tuft set as my anchor set. I then go upwind of that and put in a dirthole, or my Pipe Dream Set, something that's loud and stinky. I catch 50% of my coyotes, especially that first night, at that grass tuft. Without the dogs, I probably never would've changed my approach the way I did and started using that grass tuft as my anchor set.

RS: Do you ever move a rock or log to create a scent post?

Zagger: It's proven that coyotes are neophobic. They're suspicious of anything new in their territory, so I never move something to make a backing or a scent post. It's either already there on location or it doesn't exist, in my mind.

In 1996, I was trapping in Wyoming. The USDA was all over that area and the coyotes that were left were tough. Every time we stopped at a location, the partner I was with moved a rock or dead limb onto the road where he wanted to make a set. I just used whatever was there and out-trapped him 2 to 1. There are a lot of variables, but I think the main one was that he moved stuff around and I didn't.

RS: How well do you blend in your sets?

Zagger: When I'm done with a set, you won't even be able to tell it's there unless there's a coyote in it.

RS: How did you develop the Pipe Dream Set?

Zagger: The company that I work for owns an electrical contracting company. One day I was on a jobsite with my guys and noticed they

The pipe set works well for Mark. It is one of the sets he depends on, especially where a lot of rain is probable.

had some conduit laying across the road with extension cords running through it. It's PVC but not the white PVC you see in the plumbing section. It's that gray electrical conduit and actually pretty malleable and doesn't get brittle like the white PVC pipe. I know everybody uses white PVC for raccoon trapping, but I got to thinking about it and took a bunch of scrap pipe home from the jobsite. I thought it would be a great lure holder for coyote sets.

That summer, I had to do some nuisance trapping and decided to try the pipes. I pounded them in at a couple of sets into the grass tufts to use as a lure holder. I then made my sets the way I normally did with a deeper trap bed, a steel screen over the trap, and grass and hay clippings to blend the set in. I've actually been bedding my traps that way for almost 20 years but the pipe was a new addition. We have a lot of water in our ground here. When you dig a dirthole, it starts filling up with water as soon as you pull the auger out. So I dig my trap bed 4 to 5 inches deep and hopefully that's enough for the water to settle into and my trap just kind of floats up above it.

Anyway, I caught coyotes in those pipe sets. To this day, I've never found any books or DVDs where guys were using pipes for coyotes. So that fall, I started using it more and catching more coyotes, and I liked it. More than anything, it was a great place to stick your stink. It protected the lure and bait and made the set even more weather resistant.

I sent some pipes to a friend of mine who does videos and asked him to give them a try. He sent me footage of coyotes working the pipes. They were licking it, biting it, lying on the ground next to it trying to pull it out. I thought maybe I had something really good here.

I trap in a place that gets 100-200 inches of snow a year. The rest of the year, it rains more often than it doesn't, and I've always geared toward weather resistant methods. So I started working the pipe into my system, pounding it into tufts of grass, and in 2012, I realized just how effective it could be. That's when Hurricane Sandy hit.

Our land trapping season starts October 25th in New York. We knew that Hurricane Sandy was going to hit in one form or another on October 28th or 29th. I trap about three weeks every year, and we get so much lake effect snow in the winter, and so much rain anyway, that if I don't trap early, then I don't trap at all. I decided to change my methods and put in nothing but pipes and T-bone sets, use steel screens and grass to cover my traps, and set in nothing but hayfields.

The first few checks of the season, I caught six or seven coyotes each day. The night that Sandy hit, we got 5 inches of rain. It was devastating. All of my friends were complaining about their peat moss floating in their trap beds, dirtholes filled up with water, and they had to remake and relure everything. Meanwhile, an hour into the morning, I already had 5 coyotes in the truck. I couldn't remake anything because it was such a muddy mess. By day's end, though, I had 18 coyotes and 1 red fox. That's the best day I've ever had in New York and I don't know if I'll ever beat it.

I didn't remake or relure anything. The water went through the steel screen trap cover, my grass was still in place. The next day I caught 16 coyotes, and the day after that I caught 12. In four days, I caught 54 coyotes. The barometer dropped and animals were doing things I'd never seen them do, but I was ready for them. First, I had a lot of sets out – over 100 – and second, I had a set that was operative through all the nasty weather.

The rain washed away all the lure at the T-bone and grass tuft sets, but the pipe really protected it. Despite all that rain, the smell just settled down into the dirt inside the pipe. The scent is contained within that one-inch diameter and doesn't leech out any farther than that. I've had to leave pipes in the ground that I couldn't pull out and gone back two months later and they looked like they went through the wringer. Every animal in the countryside was probably trying to chew them up and pull them out because the scent was still in there and still working.

RS: How far should the end of the pipe stick up out of the ground?

Zagger: I think guys go wrong by leaving too much pipe sticking out of the ground or they don't use a backing. Just like my grass tuft set that I mentioned, when I walk away from one of my Pipe Dream Sets, you can't see the pipe.

RS: What's the key to putting up good numbers of coyotes?

Zagger: When guys aren't sure about location, they make up for it by setting 20 traps on a single farm. I'd rather see them spread those 20 traps across 4 or 5 farms and get on different coyotes. If you're somewhat close on location, coyotes will find your sets. You're better off not trapping against yourself and getting those traps on more coyotes – and more dumb coyotes. In the fall, 65% of the coyote population consists of first-year pups. These are not rocket scientists.

At the end of the day, with everything being equal, miles and traps are what separates the boys from the men. The more miles I run, and the more traps I run, the more I'm going to catch. We could have the same ability, but if I'm spread out over three counties and you're trapping in just one township, I'm going to beat you every time. I'm exposing my sets to more coyotes over a bigger area. Period.

For more information about Coyote U, visit Mark Zagger online at www. CoyoteU.com.

Bob Noonan, the trapper's trapper, is all smiles with his coyote catch.

Bob Noonan
Trapping Through the Years

B ob Noonan has been a household name among trappers for over 40 years. When I was an early teen in the mid-1990s and learning to trap, I sought out Noonan's articles in the various trapping magazines, not just for their educational content, but also for their entertainment value. He always had a way of teaching the reader something while making it interesting.

About that same time, I knew I wanted to be a writer, and I began clipping articles that I enjoyed and filing them away as inspiration for my own work. I think most writers do this because it's a necessary part of the learning curve – the best way learn, after all, is by emulating others who are doing what you dream of doing. It's no surprise that my collection of Bob Noonan stories quickly required a second folder.

One of my favorite Noonan articles, "Eight-Day Plan Raccoon Trapline," appeared in the September 1996 issue of Fur-Fish-Game and mapped out a simplistic approach for increasing your catch in a short period of time. I read that article dozens of times and put the methods into practice on my own trapline. Pretty soon, my catch went up, and my dad stated that I was "coonin' like Noonan." That catch phrase has stuck to this day when my dad and I talk about trapping. That's the kind of influence Noonan has had on me as a writer and as a trapper, and, I suspect, on many others like me.

Noonan is the author of countless articles and books and has produced videos on trapping marten, fishers, mink, and more. He is also the founder/owner of Trapper's Post magazine.

RS: What's your favorite species to trap?

Noonan: The older I get, the simpler I like to keep things. I don't like to drag around a lot of equipment. To me, the ultimate is blind-setting for mink with 110 bodygrips and a two-foot length of wire. There are a lot of ways to catch mink that are effective, that require equipment, but to just pin a bodygrip where I think he's going to go, that's the ultimate. I come back and see a mink in it and I go, "Ha ha ha!" You feel cocky, you know. It just feels good.

The other is fisher and marten, which are very easy to catch. But for them, it's the habitat. It's the northern Maine, fir spruce mountains, the hills, and the wilderness aspect of it that I enjoy most.

Beaver trapping can be fun, too, but it can be a pain in the butt. I'm at the age, seventy-something, that I don't like dragging a 60-pound beaver out of a bog, wearing chest waders, in 80-degree heat.

RS: You've been in the industry as a trapper, writer, and publisher for many years. How have you seen the industry change?

Noonan: That's a good question. I think our rural culture is dying. 81 or 82% of the American population is urban now. When I was a kid, everybody hunted, everybody fished. I could catch fox in high school and that was enormously prestigious. I was known as this pencil-necked geek that would ride around on his bike and kill the raccoon in your corn. I was an accepted, almost adult, member of my community. Today we're not. Today you have to hide.

I guess what's changed, for me, is that even in rural areas people have no clue about life and death and animal population dynamics. I see a real attrition among young people.

On the bureaucratic end of things, every year we come up with more and more regulations. In the fish and game departments there has been a real change. When I was a young man, in my thirties, the wardens were all outdoorsmen. They had grown up hunting and trapping. It's not that way anymore. I've had young game wardens look in the back of my truck and see a crate of 110 bodygrips and say, "What are those?"

A lot of wardens are clueless about trapping, so that's a major shift. We also have a lot of people from the cities getting their degrees in wildlife management and they have no idea how nature works.

Once, at a trappers meeting, I literally heard a biologist say that he had no problem with a father and his son going out and catching a fisher to mount and put on the mantlepiece, but this business of killing animals for profit must stop. We were dumbfounded. But here was someone who was book-trained, and he said he understood about wildlife control, such as with beaver, coyotes, and raccoons and the need to reduce animal/human conflicts, but he had no concept of wildlife as a renewable resource.

In our culture, there's a tremendous belief that animals are like people and every life is sacred. They've never seen a coyote with mange. It's a cultural war, in essence. They see man as bad and separate from nature.

RS: And if we weren't in the equation, everything would be just fine.

Noonan: That's exactly right. There's a belief among people from the city that nature will balance itself out, and if man will just get his hands off it, then wolves and moose will be friends and raccoon babies will all grow up and go to raccoon schools. Don't get me wrong, these are wonderful people who love animals, but they're clueless about nature. They haven't seen coyotes overpopulate and decimate a deer herd in the winter and then later get mange and suffer massive die-offs from disease.

RS: Who got you into trapping?

Noonan: When I was eight, we didn't have a television, so I read

Bob and his catch of flattails rest on the tailgate before going to the next location.

comic books. One day, a kid wanted to swap a Scrooge McDuck comic book for a fish trap. So, I took the trap, smashed up some clams and put it in the brackish stream, and it was full of eels the next day. The light bulb went off…why stand there holding the line when this trap sits there 24 hours a day doing its thing? Then I started thinking, why not put a minnow trap in every stream in Maine? I was a longliner at heart.

Then I learned how to live catch mice. A woman down the road had an animal farm and paid ten cents for mice. Candy bars were only a nickel. Pretty soon I was the candy bar king!

I became a trapper. It was in my blood. I just loved it and I haven't missed a season since I was nine.

The Conibear was invented when I was around 12 or 13. An article by Eric Collier in Outdoor Life claimed it was going to revolutionize trapping. I devoured it, I was so excited. Sears & Roebuck sold them in their catalog the next year for seven bucks a dozen. I mowed lawns, made money, and drove my father nuts saving up enough to get them.

There was a yellow folder that came in the box that showed four or five sets you could make, and it was incorrect because it told you to catch animals by the side of the body. First animal I caught was a skunk, by the side of the neck, and it was alive and well. I had to get my dad to come shoot it and it sprayed.

Bob with a pair of otter.

But I lived near the Scarborough Marsh, a famous muskrat spot, and Mr. Skillins lived up the road from me. He had a cellar full of hundreds of muskrat skins. It was heaven. I went down there at the age of 12, and they smelled wonderful and looked great on the stretchers. All he ever used were Blake & Lamb #1 Surehold traps. I remember showing him one of my Conibears and he said, "You know, sonny, there's been a million quack inventions and that thing will just be a flash in the pan. You wasted your money, but good for you, go and give them a try."

I started propping them in front of muskrat holes and couldn't believe how effective they were.

RS: Having grown up with very little information about trapping, what's it like to live in a day and age where information is so accessible?

Noonan: It's wonderful and it has to be this way if we want to survive. We have to educate kids. It's too easy to get discouraged. I caught my first fox as a freshman in high school by accident in a rabbit snare, but it took me years to get it. I bought books about trapping. O.L. Butcher was my hero and I followed his advice religiously.

I was in my early 30s when the fur boom of the 1970s began and fox went from $3 to $15. I stopped at a Maine Trappers Association convention and watched a fox trapping demo. I saw a guy make two sets, 15 feet apart. I'd never thought of doing that. Until then, I was only setting one trap per spot. I got an education over those two days, and before it was over, I bought four dozen 1 ½ coilsprings, and that fall I started catching doubles.

After that, I started hunting down conventions and demos. This was my family. These were guys like me, the same geeks that had the same obsession I did.

RS: Any advice for new trappers?

Noonan: Keep it simple. I'm constantly pushing to simplify, simplify, simplify, and I haven't hit the bottom yet. With coyotes, there's probably three or four pieces of equipment I use and that's it. I make a flat set. Set the trap and cover it. It's fun to blend a trap. You feel clever.

A control trapper friend of mine once said that you can't hide anything from a coyote. So forget about all the complication, the big hole, the big dirt pattern, and all that stuff. It'll catch coyotes but more and more I lean toward more simple sets like the flat set. I just like kneeling down, putting a trap in, getting up and walking away. It's the same way I trap fisher and mink.

RS: How long have you been writing trapping articles?

Noonan: I sold my first story as a professional writer in 1981 or '82 and it was about mink trapping.

I once read a story about a guy who followed around this old mink trapper. The trapper was a lifelong bachelor and jumped from motel room to motel room while running his trapline and piled up the mink along the way. He ate in restaurants. One day after dinner he went across the street and was struck and killed by a drunk driver, and a lifetime of mink knowledge was gone in an instant. That story has always stuck with me.

A lot of trappers aren't writers but they're really knowledgeable. I'm an efficient trapper, I'm adequate, but I'm good enough to recognize great ideas when I see them. As an editor, I enjoy helping other trappers share their knowledge. I'm a journalist, after all. I go out into the world and lift up a stone and see something, and then I write about it and bring it back to the tribe for their use. I'm a conduit.

And I love trapping. Even when I'm doing nuisance control work, I love catching skunks, woodchucks, or whatever. I love when I'm beaver trapping and look out there and see the hind end of a beaver floating in the water.

I'll always do it. I'll be the old man in the nursing home, and the nurses will come in and say, "Where the heck is Mr. Noonan?" I'll be down in that swamp somewhere. I'll have a 110 Conibear with a piece of wire stashed under my bed and they won't even know what it is, you know, and I'll convince them to leave it alone, it's mine. I'll be trapping until I drop.

Living in Maine, Bob is naturally a fisher trapper!

Ralph Scherder with a coyote he snared in the Florida Panhandle.